**TRAVERSE
THEATRE**

SCOTLAND'S NEW WRITING THEATRE

Traverse Theatre Company and The Ustinov, Bath
in association with Tron Theatre, Glasgow

Hoors

by Gregory Burke

cast in order of appearance

Nikki
Vick
Stevie
Tony

Director
Designer   Conor Murphy
Lighting Designer Paul Keogan
Dramaturg   Katherine Mendelsohn

Stage Manager   Gemma Smith
Deputy Stage Manager   Dan Dixon
Assistant Stage Manager Rachel Godding

**first performed at the Traverse Theatre,
Friday 1 May 2009**

a Traverse Theatre Commission

SCO+++CO   **A&B**
Arts & Business Scotland

THE TRAVERSE

Artistic Director Dominic Hill

A Rolls-Royce machine for promoting
new Scottish drama across Europe and beyond.
(The Scotsman)

The Traverse's commissioning process embraces a spirit of innovation and risk-taking that has launched the careers of many of Scotland's best-known writers including John Byrne, David Greig, David Harrower and Liz Lochhead. It is unique in Scotland in that it fulfils the crucial role of providing the infrastructure, professional support and expertise to ensure the development of a dynamic theatre culture for Scotland.

The importance of the Traverse is difficult to
overestimate . . . without the theatre, it is difficult
to imagine Scottish playwriting at all.
(Sunday Times)

From its conception in the 1960s, the Traverse has remained a pivotal venue in Edinburgh. It receives enormous critical and audience acclaim for its programming, as well as regularly winning awards. Alan Wilkins' commission for the Traverse, *Carthage Must Be Destroyed*, won Best New Play at the 2008 Critics' Awards for Theatre in Scotland. From 2001–07, Traverse Festival productions of *Gagarin Way* by Gregory Burke, *Outlying Islands* by David Greig, *Iron* by Rona Munro, *The People Next Door* by Henry Adam, *Shimmer* by Linda McLean, *When the Bulbul Stopped Singing* by Raja Shehadeh, *East Coast Chicken Supper* by Martin J Taylor, *Strawberries in January* by Evelyne de la Chenelière in a version by Rona Munro and *Damascus* by David Greig have won Fringe First or Herald Angel awards (and occasionally both). In 2008 the Traverse's Festival programme Manifesto picked up an incredible sixteen awards including a record seven Scotsman Fringe Firsts and four Herald Angels.

The most ambitious playwriting on
the Edinburgh Festival Fringe.
(New York Times)

The Traverse's success isn't limited to the Edinburgh stage. Since 2001, Traverse productions of *Gagarin Way, Outlying Islands, Iron, The People Next Door,When the Bulbul Stopped Singing*, the *Slab Boys* Trilogy, *Mr Placebo* and *Helmet* have toured not only within Scotland and the UK, but in Sweden, Norway, the Balkans, Germany, USA, Iran, Jordan and Canada. Immediately following the 2006 festival, the Traverse's production of *Petrol Jesus Nightmare #5 (In the Time of the Messiah)* by Henry Adam was invited to perform at the International Festival in Priština, Kosovo, and won the Jury Special Award for Production. During spring 2008 and 2009 the Traverse toured its award-winning 2007 production of *Damascus* to Toronto, New York, Moscow and the Middle East.

The Traverse has done Edinburgh proud.
(The Observer)

The Traverse's work with young people is of supreme importance and takes the form of encouraging playwriting through its flagship education project *Class Act*, as well as the Young Writers' Group. *Class Act* is now in its 18th year and gives school pupils the opportunity to develop their plays with professional playwrights and work with directors and actors to see the finished piece performed on stage at the Traverse. The hugely successful Young Writers' Group is open to new writers aged 18 – 25 with fortnightly meetings led by a professional playwright. Last Autumn the Traverse worked for the first time with young men from HM Young Offenders Institution Polmont to improve their literacy skills through practical drama and playwriting in a project called *OutWrite*. The participants worked with theatre professionals to develop their own plays which were performed both at HM YOI Polmont and at the Traverse.

The Traverse has an unrivalled reputation for producing contemporary theatre of the highest quality, invention and energy, and for its dedication to new writing.
(Scotland on Sunday)

The Traverse is committed to working with international playwrights and in 2005 produced *In the Bag* by Wang Xiaoli in a version by Ronan O'Donnell, the first ever full production of a contemporary Chinese play in the UK. This project was part of the successful Playwrights in Partnership scheme, which unites international and Scottish writers, and brings the most dynamic new global voices to the Edinburgh stage. Other international Traverse partnerships have included work in Québec, Norway, Finland, France, Italy, Portugal and Japan.

To find out about ways in which you can support the work of the Traverse please contact our Development Department 0131 228 3223 or development@traverse.co.uk

www.traverse.co.uk

THEATRE ROYAL BATH Ustinov

Artistic Director Andrew Smaje

The Ustinov is producing such ambitious work.
(Lyn Gardner, The Guardian)

The Ustinov is one of England's leading producers and presenters of contemporary theatre.

Recent productions include: *Gagarin Way* by Gregory Burke (directed by Lorne Campbell); *Carthage Must Be Destroyed* by Alan Wilkins (directed by Lorne Campbell); *Knives in Hens* by David Harrower (directed by Charlotte Gwinner); *Breakfast with Mugabe* by Fraser Grace (directed by Paul Robinson); *48 Hour Plays* by Kerry Hood, Tom Phillips, Peter Kesterton and Jenny Davis (directed by Andy Burden, Andrew Smaje, Sarah Dickenson and Robin Belfield); *Outlying Islands* by David Greig (directed by Loveday Ingram); *The Blue Room* by David Hare (directed by Robert Bowman); *Hilt* by Jane Bodie (directed by Andrew Smaje).

The Ustinov's writer development programme, *Script Factory*, produces more than 20 readings of new plays annually, allowing both emerging and established playwrights the opportunity to develop their latest work through both dramaturgy and intensive workshops. Writers whose work has been developed by *Script Factory* in the last year include: David Watson, Maria Roberts, Kerry Hood, Shaun McCarthy, Michael Punter and Lucinda Coxon.

The Ustinov also runs an artist development programme to nurture emerging talent in non-script-based performance. Artists and companies who have featured in Theatre Lab include: Sylvia Rimat, *Soap Soup* puppet theatre, *f.a.b. – the detonators* dance theatre, and new south west companies *Hammerpuzzle* and *Sedated by a Brick*.

Home to a major puppet festival since 2000, the Ustinov is a leading advocate for the art of object manipulation, with a particular emphasis on work for adult audiences. The Bath International Puppet Festival has showcased many UK, European and World premieres by leading international artists including: *Snuff Puppets* (Australia), *Eric Bass* (USA), Neville Tranter's *Stuffed Puppets* (Netherlands), *Les Locataires* (France), *Dude Paivia* (Brazil), alongside leading UK puppet companies *Green Ginger*, *Faulty Optic* and *Blind Summit*.

Since 2007, the Ustinov is co-host to Shakespeare Unplugged, a biennial event debunking notions of traditional Shakespeare performance, with an array of events beyond theatre buildings and across art forms. 2008 Commissions included: *Bootless Cries*, an original street dance commission based on the Sonnets from hip-hop choreographer Supple, and *7 Ages*, in which regional filmmakers made fresh stories from the Seven Ages of Man speech, in 7 new wordless films shown in found spaces across the Bath cityscape.

The Ustinov was reopened in 2008, newly designed by leading theatre architects Howarth Tompkins, whose work also includes The Young Vic, the National Theatre Studio and BAC. The Ustinov is one of the Theatre Royal Bath's three venues, which also include the award-winning *egg theatre* (also designed by Howarth Tompkins) and the historic main Theatre Royal, whose work includes many West End transfers and an annual summer season curated by Sir Peter Hall.

The Ustinov is delighted to be following its own recent revival of *Gagarin Way* (the first in England since the original Traverse/NT production in 2001) with its role as co-producer of *Hoors*.

The Ustinov Team

Andrew Smaje	Artistic Director
Chris Horseman	Chief Technician
Joe Wright	Theatre Royal Bath Technical Manager
Darren Portch	House Manager
Ed Browning	Deputy House Manager
Graeme Savage	Marketing Officer
Rosie Butcher	Graphic Designer
Anita Unwin	Wardrobe Mistress
Emma Bryant	Financial Administrator

COMPANY BIOGRAPHIES

Gregory Burke (Writer) Gregory was born in Dunfermline in 1968 and currently lives in Edinburgh. His plays include *Gagarin Way*, which was commissioned by the Traverse Theatre in association with the National Theatre Studio. It opened at the Traverse Theatre in August 2001 before transferring to the National Theatre's Cottesloe. The play won Gregory the Critics' Circle Most Promising Playwright Award and the Best New Play Award at the TMA Barclays Awards. He was also joint winner of the Meyer-Whitworth Award. The play was also nominated for the South Bank Show Theatre Award and the Laurence Olivier Award for Best New Play. Gregory's other plays include *The Straits* (Paines Plough, UK tour), *On Tour* (Royal Court Theatre/Liverpool Everyman), *Liar* (National Theatre Shell Connections) and *Black Watch* (National Theatre of Scotland, world tour). *Black Watch* won Gregory the Laurence Olivier Award for Best New Play in 2009. It also won the Writer's Guild of Great Britain Award for Best Play and the South Bank Show Theatre Award in 2007. Gregory has also adapted *Gagarin Way* and *Black Watch* for BBC Radio as well as writing original plays for radio, *Occy Eyes* and *Shellshocked*. Gregory has also written a TV drama, *Triage* for Silver River and BBC Scotland.

Andy Clark (Tony) Andy trained at RSAMD. Theatre credits include: *Tam O'Shanter* (Perth Theatre), *The Wizard of Oz* (Citizens' Theatre), *Something Wicked This Way Comes* (Catherine Wheels/ National Theatre of Scotland), *Hamlet* (Citizens Theatre), *Measure for Measure* (Clwyd Theatr Cymru), *The Seagull* (Dundee Rep), *Miss Julie* (NTS Ensemble) and *The Ching Room* (Oran Mor). For television: *Taggart, High Times* and *Missing* (SMG Productions) and *Sea of Souls* (BBC).

Jimmy Fay (Director) Jimmy is the Artistic Director of Bedrock Productions. He co-founded the Dublin Festival Fringe with Bedrock in 1995. Bedrock Productions include: *Roberto Zucco* by Bernard Marie-Koltes, *This is not a Life* by Alex Johnston, *That Time* by Samuel Beckett for Bedrock's Beckett's Ghosts at the Project Arts Centre, *Shooting Gallery* by Des Bishop and Arthur Riordan, the experimental double-bill of *Self-Accusation* and *Pale Angel* under the rubric Urban Ghosts as part of the Dublin Fringe Festival, *Faraway* by Caryl Churchill.

Jimmy's productions at the Abbey Theatre include: *Ages of the Moon* by Sam Shepard, *The Resistible Rise of Arturo Ui* by Bertolt Brecht, *The Seafarer* by Conor McPherson, *The Playboy of the Western World* in a new version by Bisi Adigun and Roddy Doyle, *Saved* by Edward Bond, *The School for Scandal* by R B Sheridan, *Howie the Rookie* by Mark O'Rowe, *True West* by Sam Shepard, Shakespeare's *Henry IV* in an edit by Mark O'Rowe, *The Muesli Belt* by Jimmy Murphy, Flánn O' Brien's *At Swim-Two-Birds* adapted by Alex Johnston and *Melonfarmer* by Alex Johnston.

Other productions include, most recently, *The Last Days of the Celtic Tiger* by Ross O'Carroll-Kelly, a Romanian version of Malachy McKenna's *Tillsonburg* at Arad State Theatre, Transylvania and Sibiu Festival, Romania, *The Chairs* by Eugene Ionesco adapted by Owen McCafferty (Tinderbox), Martin Lynch's monologue for *Convictions* (Tinderbox at Crumlin Road Jail), *True West* (Lyric Theatre), *Blown* by Nicholas Field, Royal Supreme and *Melonfarmer* by Alex Johnston (Theatre Royal, Plymouth)

Lisa Gardner (Vicky) Lisa trained at the RSAMD. Theatre includes: *The Last of the Red Hot Lovers* (Rapture Theatre); *Targets*; *Velvet Love* and *Drawing Bored* (all Glasgow Oran Mor); *Othello* and *A Midsummer Night's Dream* (both Glasgow Rep Co); *Beauty and the Beast* (Kirkcaldy Adam Smith); *Tales From Hollywood* (Perth Theatre). Other theatre credits include: *Babes in the Wood* (Kirkcaldy Adam Smith), *Whatever Happened to Baby Jane?* (Citizens' Theatre) and *Merlin The Magnificent* (Dundee Rep). For television *River City* (BBC), *Townsville* (BBC), *Sea of Souls: Amulet* (BBC), *TinselTown* (BBC). Film credits include: *Light Without Shadow* (Henry IV Wives).

Paul Keogan (Lighting Design) Paul trained at The Samuel Beckett Centre, Trinity College Dublin and at Glasgow University. For the Traverse: *Shimmer* and *Olga*. For the Abbey Theatre - *The Comedy of Errors, Ages of the Moon, Marble, The Resistible Rise of Arturo Ui, Lay Me Down Softly, Big Love, Romeo and Juliet, Woman and Scarecrow* and *Julius Caesar*. Other lighting design work includes: *The Taming of the Shrew* (Royal Shakespeare Company), *Tartuffe* (Playhouse Liverpool) *Intemperance* (Everyman, Liverpool), *Harvest* (Royal Court, London), *Blue/Orange* (Crucible, Sheffield), *Born Bad, In Arabia We'd All Be Kings* (Hampstead, London), *The Walworth Farce* (Druid), *The Deep Blue Sea, Performances, The Gates of Gold, Festen, The Old Curiosity Shop* (Gate Theatre) and *Titus Andronicus* (Siren Productions). His lighting and set design work includes *The Sugar Wife* (Rough Magic), *Trad* (Galway Arts Festival), *The Hairy Ape* and *Woyzeck* (Corcadorca), *Chair, Here Lies* (Operating Theatre), *Ballads, The Rite of Spring* (CoisCéim) and *The Massacre @ Paris* (Bedrock Productions).

Michael Moreland (Stevie) Michael trained at RSAMD. Theatre includes: *The Triumph of Love* (Royal Exchange Manchester), *Mother Goose* (Adam Smith Theatre), *What Every Woman Knows* (Royal Exchange Manchester), *Chet Baker – Speedball* (Oval House Theatre), *The Found Man* (Traverse Theatre), *Gagarin Way* (Traverse Theatre/ Royal National Theatre). Other theatre credits include: *Stroma* (Tag Theatre Co.), *Passing Places* (Greenwich & Derby), *Junk* (Oxford Stage Co.), *The Country Wife* (Bridewell Theatre), *Woof!* (Birmingham Stage Company), *Seal Wife* (Attic Theatre Company) and *Macbeth* (Chester Gateway) Television credits include: *Seven Wonders of the Industrial World – Bell Rock Lighthouse* (BBC), *Murder Prevention* (World

Productions), *The Bill* (Thames TV), *Monarch of the Glen* (Ecosse)
Casualty (BBC), *A Touch of Frost* (Yorkshire TV) and *This Life* (World
Productions). Film credits include: *New Town Killers* (NTK Films), *Sixteen
Years of Alcohol* (Tartan Films), *A Time to Love* (Hungry Eye) and *The
Trench* (Portman Films).

Conor Murphy (Set and Costume Design) Conor trained at
Wimbledon School of Art in London gaining a first class honours
degree in Theatre Design and later an MA in Scenography in Utrecht,
Holland. Conor's theatre credits include: *The Resistible Rise of Arturo Ui*,
Woman and Scarecrow, The Crucible and *The Rivals (Abbey Theatre).*
Life is a Dream, Attempts on Her Life, Dream of Autumn (Rough Magic),
The Last Days of the Celtic Tiger (Landmark Productions), *The Birthday
Party* (Bristol Old Vic), *The Playboy of the Western World, Major
Barbara* (Royal Exchange, Manchester), *Measure for Measure* (English
Touring Theatre), *Salomé* (Riverside Studios), *Summer Begins* (Donmar
Warehouse) and *The Decameron* (Gate Theatre, London). Opera credits
include: sets and costumes for *The Magic Flute* (Korean National
Opera), *Salomé* (Opéra National de Montpellier, Korean National
Opera), *The Rake's Progress* (Angers Nantes Opéra), *Powder Her Face*
(Lindbury Theatre, Royal Opera House) and *The Turn of the Screw*
(Nationale Reisopera, Holland). He has also designed sets for *Olav
Tryggvasson* (Norwegian Opera) and *Il trovatore* (English National
Opera). Designs for dance include: *The Four Seasons* (Birmingham
Royal Ballet), *Attempting Beauty* (Munich), *Giselle, Summer Night's
Dream* and *Carmen* (Donlon Dance Company, Saarbrücken).

Catherine Murray (Nikki) Catherine trained at RADA. Theatre
includes: *The Revenger's Tragedy* (The Southwark Playhouse), *Interiors –
Workshop Production* (Vanishing Point & National Theatre Studio), *Fair
Ladies At A Game Of Poem* (RADA), *Installation* (RADA), *Summerfolk*
(RADA) and *The School Mistress* (RADA). Television credits include:
New Town (Pirate Productions/BBC) and *The Marchioness* (Yorkshire
TV). Film credits include: *Tonight's the Night* (BBC).

Thank you to:

Cora Bissett, John Kazek, Samantha Young, and Roxana Silbert
for their help in workshopping the play at the Traverse in 2008

The Traverse Theatre receives financial assistance from:

The Barcapel Foundation, The Binks Trust, The Cross Trust,
The Cruden Foundation, James Thom Howat Charitable Trust,
The John Thaw Foundation, The Lloyds TSB Foundation for Scotland,
The Moffat Charitable Trust, The Peggy Ramsay Foundation,
Ronald Duncan Literary Foundation, Tay Charitable Trust,
The Thistle Trust, The Weatherall Foundation

TRAVERSE THEATRE – THE COMPANY

ARE YOU DEVOTED?

Our Devotees are: Joan Aitken, Stewart Binnie, Katie Bradford, Adrienne Sinclair Chalmers, Adam Fowler, Anne Gallacher, Keith Guy, Iain Millar, Helen Pitkethly, Michael Ridings, Bridget Stevens, Walton & Parkinson, Joscelyn Fox, Gillian Moulton, John Knight OBE

The Traverse could not function without the generous support of our patrons. In March 2006 the Traverse Devotees was launched to offer a whole host of exclusive benefits to our loyal supporters.

Become a Traverse Devotee for £29 per month or £350 per annum and receive:

- A night at the theatre including six tickets, drinks and a backstage tour

- Your name inscribed on a brick in our wall

- Sponsorship of one of our brand new Traverse 2 seats

- Invitations to Devotees' events

- Your name featured on this page in Traverse Theatre Company scripts and a copy mailed to you

- Free hire of the Traverse Bar Café (subject to availability)

Bricks in our wall and seats in Traverse 2 are also available separately. Inscribed with a message of your choice, these make ideal and unusual gifts.

To join the Devotees or to discuss giving us your support in another way, please contact our Development Department on 0131 228 3223 / development@traverse.co.uk

Charity No. SC002368

Gregory Burke
Hoors

ff

faber and faber

First published in 2009
by Faber and Faber Limited
74–77 Great Russell Street, London WC1B 3DA

Typeset by Country Setting, Kingsdown, Kent CT14 8ES
Printed in England by Bookmarque, Croyon, Surrey

A CIP record for this book
is available from the British Library

ISBN 978-0-571-25094-3

2 4 6 8 10 9 7 5 3 1

For Lisa Foster

Characters

Nikki
mid-twenties

Stevie
early thirties

Tony
early thirties

Vicky
late twenties

SCENE ONE

The living room of a house. Modern, tasteful furnishings and expensive electrical equipment. A stair, ascending, off. A door to a kitchen, off. A large shape covered with a blanket against one of the walls of the room. On that wall, a print of Titian's The Three Ages of Man. *Two women, Vicky and Nikki, sit, one on each of the two sofas. Both are very attractive and fashionably dressed. Nikki has a very small bottle of perfume in her hand. She sprays it and smells.*

Nikki I love Marc Jacobs.

Beat.

That's a man who understands what a woman wants.

Beat.

Packaging.

She picks up a small leather pouch into which the bottle of perfume fits.

The man is a fucking packaging genius.

Vicky Is he?

Nikki Average bottle of perfume comes in a box. Might be an elaborate box, but it's still just a box. Not this bloke. Box. Yeah. The box is still there. No one's seriously thinking of ditching the box. But. Inside the box. Small leather pouch with the perfume in it.

Puts the bottle back in the pouch.

A bottle, in a pouch, in a box.

7

Beat.

Genius.

She picks up a linen bag and pulls out a very expensive handbag.

I got you a bag too.

Vicky Thank you.

Nikki (*giving her the bag*) You're welcome.

Vicky This is gorgeous.

Nikki I know.

Beat.

Smell it.

Vicky (*she smells it*) Wow.

Beat.

How much was it?

Nikki You can't put a price on genius. That's what I say.

Vicky How much?

Nikki It's this season's bag.

Vicky How much?

Nikki In this season's colour.

Vicky How much?

Nikki They're cheaper over in the States.

Vicky How much?

Nikki Why are you so worried about price all of a sudden?

Vicky How much?

Pause.

Nikki One thousand . . .

Vicky Shit.

Nikki . . . nine hundred . . .

Vicky Fuck.

Nikki . . . dollars.

Vicky Are you mental?

Nikki I'm as sane as you are.

Vicky I can't take that.

Nikki Of course you can.

Vicky It's too expensive.

Nikki It's not too expensive. It's a nineteen-hundred-dollar bag. I paid nineteen hundred dollars. It was exactly the price it was.

Vicky It's still a lot of money.

Nikki It's only twelve hundred pounds.

Pause.

Vicky I can't justify having a twelve-hundred-pound bag.

Beat.

Not after what's happened.

Beat.

It'll look like I'm celebrating.

Nikki Aren't you?

Vicky No.

Pause.

And anyway, I'm not spending money like that any more.

Nikki No?

9

Vicky It's a waste.

Nikki Look I know it's a bad time, but let's not say anything we're going to regret.

She gives her the bag.

You can't complain. It was you that taught me all I know about spending money.

Beat.

You were my guru.

Vicky That's what big sisters are for.

Looks at the bag.

It is nice.

Nikki I knew it would cheer you up.

Pause.

Vicky Was I really your guru?

Nikki Course.

Beat.

It was like *The Karate Kid*. But with handbags and shoes instead of . . . karate . . . and kids.

Vicky Thank you.

They embrace.

D'you want another drink?

Nikki Yeah.

Vicky gets up.

(*Picks up a bottle from the coffee table.*) D'you want a tranquilliser?

Vicky (*offstage*) No.

Nikki (*unscrews the cap*) Sure?

Vicky Yeah.

Nikki They're really quite good, these ones.

Takes a pill from the bottle and puts it in her mouth.

I don't know why you got them if you're not going to use them?

Vicky (*comes back into the room with two glasses of wine*) I just felt I should. I didn't want to upset the doctor.

Hands Nikki a glass of wine.

You can't drink with them.

Nikki (*spits the pill out into her hand*) You sure?

Vicky It says so.

Nikki Where?

Vicky On the tin.

Nikki That's okay.

Takes a drink of her wine.

It's only a recommendation.

Takes the pill again.

And anyway, you'd buy ten pills off some dodgy bloke in a club and swallow handfuls while you're drinking, no bother. Soon as it's legal, licensed, had double-blind trials in every country in the world and we're all like, oh no, don't drink with them.

Beat.

Lot of bollocks.

Pause.

When are they coming round?

Vicky I said any time.

Nikki Any time?

Vicky Any time.

Nikki We've just got to sit here?

   Vicky shrugs.

That's good.

Vicky (*lifts her glass*) Booze.

   Shakes the bottle.

Tranquillisers.

   Beat.

What more do you want?

   Pause.

Nikki I don't see why they have to come round here tonight.

Vicky They want to see him.

   Beat.

Before tomorrow.

   Beat.

They're his friends.

Nikki They were his friends.

   Pause.

Sorry. I didn't mean that. I mean . . . you know what his friends are like?

Vicky They're not that bad.

   Pause.

Nikki So, it's an evening listening to a bunch of idiots talking about when they used to have waists?

Vicky They're his friends.

Pause.

Nikki I can't believe you were getting married to a builder.

Vicky You can't go wrong with bricks and mortar.

Nikki Didn't you tell me never to go out with someone without a degree?

Vicky Well, you know what our gran used to say?

Nikki Don't talk romantic?

Vicky There's no point in trying to force children to learn.

Beat.

Mrs Hutchison that had the post office tried to make her girl learn and we all know what happened to her . . .

Nikki Alopecia.

Vicky Alopecia.

Nikki Was that not depression, though?

Vicky She never had depression, she went to university.

Pause.

I could've gone to university.

Beat.

I just preferred discos.

Nikki You were very good at them, I heard.

Vicky I was.

Nikki We could go to a disco tonight?

Vicky No we can't.

Nikki We can.

Vicky I want to see Stevie.

Nikki Has he been coming round here a lot?

Vicky Yeah.

Nikki People will talk.

Vicky Yeah.

Nikki With their mouths.

Vicky (*shrugs*) People better get used to it.

Nikki Something you haven't told me?

Vicky We have an understanding.

Nikki An understanding?

Vicky An understanding.

Nikki Which is?

Vicky If anything ever happened to . . . (*Indicates coffin.*) we would . . .

Nikki I thought he was married.

Vicky That's all over.

Nikki People say funny things to people who are grieving. They don't know what to say.

Vicky We have an understanding.

Nikki You do know people won't be very understanding about an understanding like that?

Vicky That's their problem.

Nikki It's their problem?

Vicky If people don't like the way I behave that's their problem.

Nikki That's the problem.

Vicky What?

Nikki Historically . . . that's not a good position to take.

Pause.

So what's been going on?

Vicky Nothing. So far. Just talking.

Beat.

We love talking to each other.

Always have. Always got along.

Pause.

And we've had sex.

Nikki When?

Vicky The night he – (*Indicates coffin.*) told me the news.

Nikki Blimey.

Pause.

And how was that?

Vicky It was . . . nice.

Nikki Oh.

Puts her hand on Vicky's arm.

Never mind.

Vicky What?

Nikki Nice isn't good.

Vicky Yes it is.

Beat.

It's . . . nice.

Pause.

He's got feelings for me. That's what he says.

Nikki Does he not know how shit that sounds?

Pause.

Have you ever thought he might be after your money?

Vicky What money?

Nikki I mean. (*Indicates surroundings.*) He'd be on a good thing here.

Vicky Don't let this fool you, sis. This is all an illusion.

Pause.

His heart's in the right place.

Nikki Shame.

Vicky Anyway, that mate of Andy is coming. Tony.

Nikki Who?

Vicky One of his mates.

Beat.

I've never met him. They used to work together when they were younger. He's come all the way from . . . he lives somewhere . . . abroad.

Beat.

Somewhere.

Nikki We should get out of their way and let them catch up.

Vicky He's very nice.

Nikki I'm sure he is.

Vicky No. I mean he's nice.

Nikki Really?

Vicky Really nice.

Nikki Have you met him?

Vicky I once saw a photo.

Nikki You can't trust a photo.

Vicky He's really quite braw.

Nikki We should probably stay and say hello then?

Vicky You think?

Nikki Best to, really.

Beat.

He has come a long way.

Pause.

D'you want to put the telly on?

Vicky No.

Nikki How about some music?

Pause.

Vicky I have met him once, actually.

Nikki Who?

Vicky Tony.

Beat.

His pal that's coming here.

Nikki Oh, right.

Pause.

Vicky I say 'met him', obviously I mean in the sense that we fucked each other senseless.

Nikki Oh . . . that sense.

Vicky Just the once.

Nikki That's a good sense.

Vicky It is.

Nikki When was that? When you were . . . (*Indicating coffin.*) with . . .

Vicky No.

Beat.

Not with . . . just that bit . . .

That grey bit . . .

Nikki Pre-exclusivity?

Vicky Is that bad?

Nikki You've got to keep your options open.

Vicky I was always very open with my options.

Pause.

I don't think about it much.

Nikki No?

Vicky No.

Nikki Good.

Vicky It's just one of those fucks that's always going to be there. In your . . .

Nikki Head.

Vicky Always.

Pause.

You know what I'm not looking forward to?

Nikki What's that?

Vicky The sympathy.

Beat.

I fucking hate sympathy.

Nikki It's inevitable.

Vicky I hate it.

Nikki It's out of your hands.

Vicky This is going to be the thing that people will define me by.

Nikki Definitely.

Vicky All I'll be is a widow, his widow, from now on. And every year it'll be the same thing. The same conversation. Christmas and birthdays. Every single year. The same conversation about the same things. It's going to be so fucking boring.

Nikki You could always run away?

Vicky Not in these shoes I couldn't.

Pause.

I'm fucked now.

Nikki Doesn't matter what you do. Move on: slut. Don't move on: tragic.

Beat.

You're fucked.

Vicky I'm fucked.

Nikki You're fucked.

Beat.

Promise me one thing though ay.

Vicky What's that?

Nikki (*rattles the bottle of tranquillisers*) Don't top yourself.

Vicky Don't be daft.

Nikki It's silly.

Vicky It's stupid.

Nikki gets up and wanders over to the shape that is obscured against the wall.

Nikki Did you think that they looked shocked earlier?

Vicky Who?

Nikki I thought the guy who first came in with the stand looked a bit shocked.

Vicky Why would he be shocked?

Nikki That you were so young.

Vicky joins Nikki at the far wall of the room.

Vicky They must see things like this all the time.

Nikki gets up and wanders over to the shape that is obscured against the wall.

Nikki I'm still not sure about having to have him back here.

Vicky joins Nikki and pulls the cover off to reveal a coffin on a stand.

Vicky It's traditional.

Nikki It's creepy.

Vicky (*folds up the cover and puts it down*) It's okay for you, you don't have to do anything. I'm going to have to act like I'm upset. Play the grieving widow.

Beat.

And, technically, I'm not even a widow.

(*To the coffin.*) Fucking idiot.

Beat.

Have you ever heard of anyone dying on their stag night?

Nikki I'm sure it's more common than you think.

Vicky Getting buried on the day they were supposed to be getting married?

Nikki At least you had the church booked.

Vicky (*to the coffin*) Arse.

Nikki (*goes to Vicky and puts her arm round her*) Come on.

Vicky Well . . . it's so fucking . . .

Nikki Inconvenient?

Vicky Embarrassing.

Beat.

People have gone to a lot of expense. The presents . . .

Nikki Don't worry about the presents. No one will have bought you anything nice.

Vicky I don't know if I can face everybody.

Nikki You can.

Beat.

People'll understand.

Pause.

And have you ever been to a good wedding?

Vicky Yeah.

Nikki I've never been to a good wedding.

Vicky You don't like weddings?

Nikki Weddings are shit.

Vicky No they're not.

Nikki Have you ever been to a good one?

Vicky Loads.

Nikki Whose?

Vicky Eh . . .

Nikki I mean a proper good one where you stood there and said, I can see the point of this, I can see what they mean here. I can see why they would want to do this.

Beat.

Folk have to fork out a grand just for the privilege of being there. New dress, new shoes, new bag, new hair. Diet for a month. Hotel. Present. Drink and drugs to numb the boredom. 'S fucking rubbish.

Beat.

By tomorrow night it'll all be over.

Vicky That still leaves twenty-four hours.

Nikki You can do it.

Vicky Telling me how nice a guy he was. How much they liked him.

Nikki It's what happens.

Vicky Expecting me to be distraught.

Beat.

Them pretending to be distraught.

Nikki Lie.

Vicky I don't like lying.

Nikki So tell the truth.

Vicky No.

Nikki You've no option. Come on, let's run through it.

She pulls Vicky to her feet.

I'm the cliché-spouting person who hasn't seen either of us for years.

Vicky Right.

Nikki (*takes a breath*) How are you feeling?

Vicky Hang on.

Beat.

Which side?

Nikki What?

Vicky Which side? Of the family?

Nikki Oh, right.

Beat.

Well, who's going to be, I mean, our side. Has to be. He doesn't really have anyone left.

Vicky No.

Nikki He only had his mates.

Beat.

And you.

Vicky Stop it.

Nikki Sorry.

Vicky You're making me feel sorry for him.

Nikki So I'm Auntie somebody from some-fucking-where . . .

Pause.

How are you feeling, hen?

Vicky I'm . . .

Nikki When my Tam died, oh, I never had anybody . . . except the bairns, and his sisters . . . and my mum and –

Vicky What the fuck is that?

Nikki It's Auntie Hingy.

Vicky No. I mean, what was all that stuff about Tam? Who's Tam?

Nikki Her husband.

Beat.

He died . . .

Vicky Who died?

Nikki Auntie Hingy's husband.

Pause.

I thought it was quite good.

Vicky (*shakes her head*) You need to stop taking those tranquillisers.

Nikki You need to tell folk how you feel.

Pause.

How are you feeling, hen?

Vicky Em . . . well . . . relieved, I suppose.

Nikki Relieved?

Vicky Yeah, really fucking relieved.

Nikki Well, he didnay suffer at least.

Vicky No. I mean I'm really relieved I'm not having to get married. The spark had gone. The second wind had blown itself out. Would've been a huge mistake.

Beat.

Don't think I loved him.

Nikki You can't say that.

Vicky You said be honest.

Nikki Not to me.

Vicky You're my sister.

Nikki I'm Auntie fucking Hingy.

Vicky You see this is what I fucking mean. I'm no good at this stuff.

Pause.

Nikki (*still as Auntie Hingy*) Just say to yourself, they're just in the next room.

Vicky What?

Nikki They've just moved next door.

Vicky Who has?

Nikki (*indicates coffin*) Him.

Vicky Who?

Nikki You have to say that you're telling yourself that they've just moved.

Vicky Where?

Nikki I don't know where.

Vicky Next door?

Nikki Yeah.

Vicky Mrs McJagger lives next door?

Nikki You say they've moved so you don't have to say they're dead. (*Points to the coffin.*) He's moved away to . . .

Vicky A tiny, wee underground flat?

Nikki Yes.

Vicky In a cemetery?

Nikki Exactly.

Vicky (*smiles*) That's a relief.

Nikki And since when was relief one of the five stages of grief?

Vicky I don't know.

Nikki Come on, we went through the five stages of grief earlier . . .

   Beat.

Shock.

Vicky Shock.

   Beat.

Horror?

Nikki Sorrow.

Vicky Sorrow . . .

   Pause.

Hysteria?

Nikki Anger.

Vicky Anger.

Beat.

Sexual frustration?

Nikki Apathy and depression. Recovery. You are fucking hopeless.

Vicky I know. It's going to be a disaster.

Beat.

What am I going to do?

Nikki Strict adherence to social norms and expectations and everythings gonnay be alright.

Beat.

The five stages of grief. Shock. Sorrow. Anger. Apathy and depression. Recovery.

Beat.

Or in your case. Lie. Lies. Lying. Untruths. And . . .

Vicky Falsehoods?

Nikki If you do anything wrong, it's 'cause you're in shock. If you cry, it's sorrow. If you punch anyone, it's anger. If you fall asleep, it's depression. If you happen to get tipsy and get off with someone, it's recovery. There's no set time period for the five stages. They might all happen in one day.

Pause.

Now come on.

Vicky I can't be bothered.

Nikki See, apathy and depression.

Beat.

Now let's have another drink.

27

She gets up.

I've no sympathy for you. This should all have been nipped in the bud a long time ago.

Vicky Well, I'm prone to letting things drift.

Nikki It's one thing letting things drift, it's another to end up married to them.

Vicky He asked me.

Nikki You could have just said no.

Vicky He caught me off guard.

Beat.

I mean his dad had just died.

Beat.

He didn't have anybody else.

Beat.

And the closer it got.

Beat.

He was looking forward to it that much.

Nikki Sad bastard.

Vicky (*shouts*) You're talking about the man I loved!

Pause.

Nikki Now that was good.

Vicky It was, wasn't it?

Nikki Very convincing.

Vicky I think I felt something?

Nikki Keep that up and you're laughing.

Beat.

You know, you've been lucky in a way.

Vicky Lucky?

Nikki At least he didn't leave you. That would have been really embarrassing.

Vicky At least if he'd left me he would have taken his stuff.

The doorbell rings.

Vicky I think I might love him.

Nikki Who?

Vicky Stevie.

Nikki No you don't!

The doorbell rings again.

Vicky We better get him on display.

Nikki You do it, I'll get the door.

Nikki exits. Vicky opens the lid of the coffin.

Vicky Arse.

SCENE TWO

Living room. Nikki and Vicky have been joined by Tony and Stevie.

Stevie It's impossible to say anything at a time like this.

Vicky No, it isn't.

Nikki It's only impossible to say the right thing.

Pause.

Tony Can I just say how sorry I am?

Vicky Thank you.

Tony It must be such a difficult time.

Vicky Yes.

Stevie There's nothing can prepare anyone for something like this.

Nikki No.

Tony No.

Vicky No.

  Beat.

There isn't.

(*To Tony.*) And it's really nice to meet you.

Tony Ay?

Vicky At long last.

Tony Eh . . . yeah.

  Beat.

Nice to meet you. Too.

  Pause.

Nikki We're all just so shocked.

Stevie I mean, what do you do?

Vicky What can you do?

Nikki Time.

Tony Time.

Vicky Time.

Stevie Time?

Tony Time's the only . . .

Nikki Healer.

Vicky Yes.

   Beat.

Time.

Stevie (*to Vicky*) D'you think?

   Beat.

I mean . . . aye. It's the only . . . healer . . . time.

   Pause.

Tony It's a tragedy. That's the only word I can think of.

   Beat.

Tragic.

   Long pause.

Stevie Can I just say, before I say anything else, and despite the circumstances and that, you're both looking . . . lovely . . . this evening.

   Pause.

Vicky (*to Tony*) When did you get back?

Tony I came straight from the airport.

Nikki (*to Tony*) Where did you come from?

Tony Dubai.

Vicky Nice.

Tony I like it.

Vicky You must be tired.

Tony A little bit.

Nikki Are you back for long?

Tony Just for the . . .

Nikki Tomorrow?

Tony Yes.

Nikki It's a funeral.

Tony Yeah.

Nikki In case you're confused.

Pause.

Vicky Would anyone like a drink? What would you like, Tony?

Tony A beer, eh? Cheers. Thanks.

Vicky What sort?

Tony Anything.

Vicky Stevie?

Stevie No.

Vicky No?

Stevie I'm not drinking at the minute.

Tony No?

Stevie No.

Tony Since when?

Stevie Since the . . . eh . . . stag night.

Tony Aye?

Stevie Aye.

Beat.

If you'd been there you'd understand.

Vicky exits.

Nikki (*calls after her*) I'll have another.

Stevie How is she?

Nikki Well, it's early days.

Tony Too soon to say?

Nikki Aye.

Tony She'll be in shock.

Nikki I think so.

Stevie Absolutely.

Nikki Shock's the first stage.

Stevie I remember when my mum died. The shock.

Nikki It's a terrible shock.

Stevie Aye.

Beat.

'Cause our dad had telt us she was already dead ay.

Pause.

Tony (*to Nikki*) It'll be a long slow process for her.

Nikki It'll take time.

Tony Time. It's the only . . . thing.

Pause.

It's just all so . . .

Nikki I know.

Tony Such a . . .

Nikki It is. It is.

Vicky enters with drinks.

Vicky If you want to see him. Feel free.

Stevie and Tony turn towards the coffin.

Nikki Do you want us to leave you alone?

Tony No. No.

Stevie We're fine.

Nikki You sure?

Stevie Of course.

Vicky We should stay.

Stevie You should.

Vicky It's only right.

Stevie Stay.

Tony and Stevie go over to the coffin and look in.

Tony It's just like he's sleeping.

Stevie D'you think?

Tony Yes.

Beat.

I do.

Pause.

He looks so young?

Vicky He was young.

Pause.

Tony I like what they've dressed him in.

Beat.

Very smart.

Vicky Thanks.

Stevie We were all going to be wearing that.

Tony Were you?

Stevie Aye.

Tony Really?

Stevie Aye.

Pause.

Tony That would have been very . . . smart.

Nikki You should see her dress.

(*To Vicky.*) Go and get your dress and let them see it.

Vicky No.

Nikki Go on, you should.

Vicky No. I don't . . .

Nikki She looks so beautiful in it. You should see her.

Pause.

Vicky So what have you got planned while you're at home, Tony?

Tony Nothing much.

Stevie A night out with the boys.

Vicky Going to lead him astray, are you?

Tony Not if I can help it.

Stevie (*to Tony*) You will have time for a night out with the lads, though?

Nikki (*to Tony*) Lucky you.

Stevie You will though ay?

Tony Maybe.

Beat.

What have you got in mind?

Stevie Oh the usual ay . . . Why fight it? That's my motto. Get yourself up the town, get blind drunk and secure some sexual congress with an errant teen.

Tony I think I'll maybe give that a miss.

Stevie You wouldnay have said that a few years ago.

Tony I must have changed.

Stevie He was unbelievable.

Nikki Were you?

Tony It's all a long time ago.

Nikki It'll maybe come back to you when you go out?

Stevie He maybe doesn't want to go out in case he bumps into any ghosts from his past.

Vicky Town this size, you can't help but bump into ghosts.

Tony (*to Stevie*) Aye, so how is your wife anyway?

Pause.

Fucking joker ay. Till anycunt mentions that.

Vicky Now now, boys. Let's not fall out.

Nikki Did your wife ever get that restraining thing on you, Stevie? It was a hundred yards or something, wasn't it?

Vicky It was metres?

Nikki Is the legal system metric?

Stevie It's two hundred feet.

Tony How does that work for picking up the bairn? Does she have tay, like, catapult him tay you?

Stevie I dinnay get tay see the bairn any more.

Pause.

Vicky At least you never ended up in jail.

Tony You were lucky.

Nikki Stalking's a serious thing nowadays.

Stevie I wasnay stalking her, I was trying to give her back some of her stuff.

Nikki At four in the morning?

Stevie Aye.

Vicky I don't know why you didn't just plead temporary insanity?

Stevie Well, I wasnay really thinking straight ay.

Pause.

Vicky (*smiles at Stevie*) Where did it all go wrong?

Tony He hates women, that's his problem.

Stevie I dinnay hate women.

Tony Aye you do.

Stevie I don't.

Vicky I think I might go for a bit of a lie-down.

Nikki Are you?

Vicky (*to Tony and Stevie*) You don't mind?

Tony Of course not.

Stevie You go and get some rest.

Vicky exits up the stairs.

(*Looks at the coffin.*) I still say we should have taken him out.

Nikki You wanted to take him out?

Stevie I've always wanted tay take a dead body out for a drink.

Pause.

Have you seen him?

Nikki I don't want to see him.

Stevie No?

Nikki No.

Stevie He looks fine.

Nikki I don't care.

Stevie If anything he looks slightly better than he did when he was alive.

Pause.

Is Vicky putting anything in the coffin with him?

Nikki I don't think so.

Stevie We should maybe stick something in with him. For the afterlife.

Nikki He's getting cremated.

Pause.

Stevie I think that's a shame.

Beat.

He's no' even gonnay get the chance to be a skeleton.

Tony (*to Nikki*) Are you wanting another drink?

Stevie (*to Nikki*) Do you ever think about being a skeleton?

Nikki (*to Tony*) Oh yes.

Tony exits to the kitchen.

Stevie I think your skeleton would look nice.

Pause.

Nikki Okay.

Stevie Does that sound creepy?

Beat.

I dinnay want it tay sound creepy.

Nikki Well you need to not say it then.

Stevie All I mean is that . . .

Nikki Ever.

Stevie What I mean is that, like, people place all this importance on like skin and hair and eyes and stuff. Fat and muscle. But the main basis for our structure, for the way we look, is the bones.

Beat.

They're the foundations.

Beat.

So really if you're seeing beyond all the superficial stuff. All the outside stuff. The layers. All the skin and hair and eyes and stuff. Fat and muscle. Like people want us to. Then you really should be appreciating the bones.

Nikki It isn't getting any less creepy.

Stevie My favourite bone's the pelvic bone.

Tony returns with the drinks. He hands one to Nikki.

Nikki You know what I think?

Stevie What?

Nikki I think somebody needs tay dig up your back garden.

39

Stevie I stay in a flat.

Nikki So what do you do with the bodies?

Tony I told you he's always hated women?

Stevie No, I don't.

Nikki (*to Stevie*) You sound like you do.

Stevie I put that down to my grandad.

Nikki Was he a woman?

Stevie He was a bastard. A horrible man. Not tay me like. He loved me. But he was a real grade-A woman-hater. When we were little, you know, we used to watch films and stuff – you know, when I was staying with him and my gran at weekends and stuff. We'd sit there, Saturday afternoon, some daft war film on, or a cowboy or something, John Wayne, and as soon as the first woman appeared on screen up he'd get. Big sigh. That's the picture finished he'd say, there's a woman in it. An' he'd turn it over. I used to say to him, what's wrong and he'd say, there's a woman in it. It's ruined, they're no' gonnay do anything now. Women spoil everything. Come on, we'll watch the wrestling, Mick McManus is on.

Nikki That's terrible.

Stevie I'm just glad I've never allowed that sort of attitude to rub off on me.

Nikki You have to be very strong to rebel against your early socialisation.

Stevie Yeah.

   Beat.

That's right.

Nikki We all have to reject the patriarchal strictures that society tries to impose.

Stevie I was just saying that to T.

Tony (*to Nikki*) He was, you know. He also made several points about the objectification of women.

   Pause.

Nikki Youse are full of shit.

Tony We're all full of shit, darling. Youse just have better PR than us.

Stevie It's like dolphins.

Nikki Dolphins?

Tony Or the Dalai Lama.

Stevie Everybody goes on about how they're all fucking lovely.

Nikki They are.

Stevie They're no'.

Nikki Excuse me. I was in Florida once. And I can tell you that, having swum with dolphins. They're great.

Stevie Iraq.

Nikki Iraq?

Stevie Dolphins were involved in the Iraq war.

Nikki Which dolphins?

Stevie I dunno which dolphins. But dolphins were involved in the invasion of Iraq.

Nikki Not my dolphin.

Stevie But dolphins.

Nikki He was lovely. He pulled me along on his back.

Stevie There's a team of them in the US Marines. I mean, we slag the Yanks and that ay, for their aggressive fucking posture in the world, but not one person has stood up and said fuck these dolphin cunts and their imperialist work. They're quick enough to get themselves in the papers when they've been leading some swimmer to safety, protecting babies from sharks and that. But not a word about their covert military operations.

Beat.

Dolphins? They don't give a fuck who they take their fish from.

Nikki Who knew?

Stevie I thought you might have? What with your line of work?

Nikki I didn't. But then the western military industrial complex is a broad church.

Nikki exits.

Stevie What has the Dalai Lama ever done?

Tony No fucker's that nice.

SCENE THREE

Living room. Tony and Stevie stand looking into the open lid of the coffin.

Stevie Horrible.

Tony Fucking horrible.

Stevie I ken.

Pause.

Tony Vile.

Stevie Aye.

Pause.

Tony Fucking vile.

Pause.

Tony (*pointing into the coffin*) What the fuck is that shite?

Stevie Aye.

Tony There's no way I'd wear something like that tay get buried in.

Stevie No fucking way.

Pause.

Tay be fair, he didn't actually get it tay get buried in ay. He was supposed tay be getting married in it ay.

Tony It's still fucking horrible, though?

Stevie Oh aye, it's fucking horrible.

Tony I just dinnay get it way these things like. It's wrong for every fucking occasion.

Stevie Can you believe he fucking bought it tay?

Tony I cannay.

Stevie They're like, a fucking grand or something ay.

Tony Fuck's sake.

Stevie He didnay even like fucking kilts.

Tony He used tay always go on about how much he hated them.

Stevie He'd never been further north than fucking Perth in his life.

Pause.

Tony And you were going tay be dressed like that?

Stevie Aye.

Tony Fuck.

Stevie (*nods*) Aye.

Tony Lucky fucking escape.

Pause.

Who's he supposed tay be?

Stevie He's no' supposed tay be anyone.

Tony Is he like Rob Roy?

Stevie A wee bit.

Tony William Wallace?

Stevie I think it's . . . it's like a mixture ay Rob Roy and William Wallace.

Tony Robbie Williams?

Stevie picks up a bottle of beer and takes a long drink.

I thought you werenay drinking?

Stevie That was just for the lassies.

Tony Aye?

Stevie Discipline impresses people nowadays.

They take a drink and look into the coffin.

Tony Is the kilt supposed tay be that short?

Stevie I dinnay ken.

Tony It's like a fucking mini?

Stevie It's maybe shrunk or something?

Tony How the fuck would it shrink?

Stevie Do they not pump stuff intay you when you're dead? Or something.

Beat.

He's maybe expanded?

Pause.

He pumped plenty stuff intay his veins in the Dam anyway.

Tony So it was a good weekend?

Stevie Carnage, mate. Fucking bloodbath. Hamburg for a night, Amsterdam for a night. It's one ay the best stag nights I've ever been on in my life.

Tony Bastard.

Beat.

I knew I should have gone.

Stevie Aye.

Beat.

How didn't you go?

Tony It's a long way to come to get drunk and fuck a prostitute.

Beat.

I get enough ay that at home.

Stevie Too many people are too quick tay cite Amsterdam as Europe's most depraved city, but you overlook Hamburg at your peril.

Tony The groom having a fucking heart attack must hay taken the shine off ay things though ay?

Stevie Tay be fair, it was beginning to wind down by then.

Tony So what exactly happened?

Stevie It was on the Sunday ay, so we'd, ken, we'd really been out on one ay. We'd got these adrenalin pills off ay this Indonesian bloke.

Tony An Indonesian bloke?

Stevie Aye. (*Shrugs.*) Fay Jakarta.

Tony That already doesnay sound good.

Stevie Little tiny dwarf cunt.

Tony It's no' getting any better.

Stevie What?

Tony You bought adrenalin pills off an Indonesian dwarf?

Stevie He said they were herbal speed.

Tony Herbal speed?

Stevie He said they'd keep us going.

Tony Herbal fucking speed?

Stevie He wasnay fucking joking.

Tony He was tiny but he was right?

Stevie We were all fucked ay, but we wanted tay keep going. Andy takes a couple ay the wee dwarfy boy's pills. But they're no' having an effect. So he has another couple, and another couple and . . .

   Beat.

Fucking herbal speed? Bollocks.

   Beat.

Pure fucking adrenalin in pill form. Stop your heart fucking dead. He collapsed right outside the Van Gogh Museum.

Tony The Van Gogh Museum?

Stevie They do a good breakfast.

   Pause.

The doctors were amazed he survived.

Tony He didnay survive.

Stevie He survived the first heart attack. But he discharged himself from the hospital and got a taxi tay the airport. Everyone was falling about the place thinking it was hysterical. He still had the wee rubber things fay the heart monitors stuck all over him ay. Everybody was killing themselves ay and we were sitting on the plane, an' he kept like fucking bending over an' that ay. Massaging his chest an' stuff. It was like he had indigestion.

Beat.

Then he went tay the toilet and . . .

Pause.

He must have bumped intay the stewardess on the way.

Tony The stewardess?

Stevie That he was in the toilet with when his heart . . .

Tony Fuck.

Stevie I couldnay understand it.

Tony I thought he was already in the mile-high club?

Stevie No' on a budget airline though ay.

Tony It'd be rude not to at those prices.

Stevie (*takes a drink*) Poor . . . Vicky.

Tony You ken what he was like.

Stevie Aye, but your fiancé dies on his stag night from a stewardess-induced heart attack in the toilet ay a plane and has tay get buried on your wedding day.

Tony How do I miss a fucking escapade ay this fucking quality?

Stevie It's never gonnay be fucking bettered.

47

Tony I ken.

Stevie Important thing is, Vicky kens nothing about it.

Tony She doesnay ken?

Stevie No.

Tony How the fuck?

Stevie It was agreed.

Beat.

And she's never gonnay ken about it.

Tony Absolutely.

Pause. Lifts his drink.

Tay Big Andy.

Stevie What a guy.

Tony Some boy.

Stevie Some cunt.

Tony Aye.

Stevie Oh aye.

Tony Fuck aye.

Stevie By fuck aye.

Pause.

No advance?

Tony No.

Stevie Thank fuck.

Tony We'd be here all fucking night.

Pause.

Nice coffin though ay?

Stevie Really nice.

Tony The Co-op are fucking brilliant these days.

Stevie It's from their designer range?

Tony Pour Corpse?

They laugh.

Stevie Good tay see you though, mate.

Tony Likewise.

Pause.

Cannay believe he's dead, though. Can you?

Stevie I suppose if you saw him ay.

Dying.

Tony I always thought he was indestructible.

Stevie I ken, but he was really caning it ay.

Tony I thought he'd given up all that?

Stevie He had.

Tony Last time I spoke to him, he was telling me about how he was getting back in shape for his big day.

Stevie Special occasion though ay.

Tony Aye.

Stevie Like today.

Tony Aye. Come on, get on the phone to your man.

Stevie Nay need.

Removes a cellophane bag from his pocket and waves it in Tony's face.

I brought a little bit ay personal back fay the Dam. If you cannay hay a bit today, when can you?

Tony It's what he would have wanted.

Stevie That's probably what the fucking problem was, the reason for him being in there. Fucking abstinence. It's fucking fatal. Starts getting all fit and no going out and being a fucking boring cunt and then when the time comes for a blow out –

Begins to pour the cocaine onto the top of the coffee table.

Your body cannay cope.

Tony So don't fucking stop.

Holds up his bottle.

Tay Amsterdam.

Stevie (*lifts his drink*) Tay the Van Gogh Museum.

Tony Van Gogh.

They clink their glasses and take a drink.

Stevie Fucking nineteenth-century, self-harming Orange fuck.

Stevie produces a credit card from his wallet and starts chopping.

Tony Now the party's starting.

Tony bends down and snorts a line of cocaine. Stevie also bends and snorts a line.

Stevie (*sniffing*) Officially, under fucking way.

They both drink.

So how are you?

Tony I'm fine.

Stevie Still doing the . . .

Tony (*nods*) Still.

Stevie And how's that these days?

Tony You see it all.

Stevie I can imagine.

Tony See it fucking all.

Pause.

How about you?

Stevie Me?

Tony Aye.

Stevie Grand. Aye . . . grand.

Tony Still?

Stevie Aye.

Tony Good . . . good.

Pause.

And how are you about all this?

Stevie Fine.

Beat.

Fine.

Tony Are you?

Stevie It's a shock an' that ay, dinnay get me wrong. But, ken, we were at that point ay his life, our lives, where I wasn't really going tay see much of him again anyway. Marriage would have removed him from the equation ay my life.

51

Tony Your life's an equation these days?

Stevie Well . . .

Tony What the fuck-fucking equation is that, then?

Stevie I'm not really sure which exact equation it is, ken, like but –

Tony Like a maths equation?

Stevie Eh . . .

Tony Something fay quantum mechanics? String theory? Which equation exactly is it like?

Pause.

You've no' really thought this through, have you?

Stevie I havenay thought it through, no.

Tony You should always think things through, pal.

Stevie Aye.

Pause.

What d'you think ay Vicky?

Tony Nice.

Stevie Aye.

Tony I prefer the sister.

Stevie Fuck aye.

Beat.

Goes without saying.

Tony That's a very nice-looking girl.

Stevie Stuck up a wee bit.

Tony Was she?

Stevie No' tay you ay. You're a novelty. Tay me.

Tony You're familiar.

Stevie Contempt's what I'm gonnay get.

Tony Quite right too.

   Pause.

Stevie Vicky, though?

Tony What about her?

Stevie It's kinday difficult tay put it right.

Tony What?

Stevie Well.

   Beat.

Right.

   Beat.

Well, you know, what with him dying an' that ay . . .

Tony Aye.

Stevie Well, you know, Vicky . . .

Tony Aye.

Stevie Well, Vicky . . .

Tony Fuck's sake, spit it out.

Stevie I mean, I ken she'll be pretty vulnerable an' that ay? I mean, I ken that ay.

Tony Aye.

Stevie She'll no' be feeling herself?

Tony Aye.

Stevie She'll be in shock.

Tony First stage ay grief. Shock.

Stevie But, well . . . it's funny though ay. I've always got on really well with her ay . . .

Tony Aye?

Stevie And like, I mean, well, she always said, like, ken, you know, like if anything, ken, ever happened, like to me and . . . the wife –

Tony Lyndsey.

Stevie Aye, and like the big fella, ken, like, and she was joking at the time, dinnay get me wrong, I ken she was joking and that ay . . . but she used tay say, she always used tay say . . . anything happens to those two, it's you and me.

Tony Aye?

Stevie And I'm no' being funny or anything, and I ken this might sound strange, but I dinnay think she's that bothered about Andy.

Tony Bollocks.

Stevie I'm telling you.

Tony How the fuck can she be no' bothered?

Stevie All I'm saying is . . . I notice stuff.

Tony Fuck off. Come on. If you're deluding yourself that you're in there, that's fine. But dinnay make out it's her.

Stevie I'm fucking telling you.

Tony Have you been laying it on really thick?

Stevie Laying what on really thick?

Tony Anything I can do.

Beat.

Anything.

Beat.

And I mean anything.

Beat.

Just ask.

Pause.

And has she asked?

Stevie Well, ay . . . no' really ay . . . like, talked about it ay. But, ken, I kinday get this feeling she wants to. Ask.

Pause.

Tony Well they do say that until you fuck a woman who's grieving or pregnant you haven't lived.

Stevie Who says that?

Tony Me.

Beat.

Just there the now.

Pause.

Stevie D'you think folk would be fine about it though?

Tony Hypothetically?

Stevie Aye?

Tony What do I suppose constitutes a reasonable interlude before you should hit on her?

Stevie Aye?

Tony I reckon you should at least let her get through the funeral first.

Stevie Obviously.

Tony Sexy things, though, funerals.

Stevie Aye, they do tend tay fucking concentrate the mind.

Tony We're all gonnay end up in that fucking box one day so get your fucking pants off.

Stevie Even better than weddings.

Tony No' with the fucking widow, though.

Stevie She's no' a fucking widow.

Beat.

Or his fucking wife.

Pause.

I dinnay ken what you're being so fucking moral about anyway. Fuck's sake. You cannay give the fucking talk on sexual morality tay any cunt.

Tony I can't, no, you're right. But I've heard a lot ay stuff about people in these situations. Sometimes they go the other way. Women lose their men, become lesbians. Blokes whose wives die become double adaptors.

Stevie Fuck off.

Tony It's maybe because they cannay replace the other person or because they were anyway and now they're free.

Beat.

Whose tay say?

Pause.

Stevie That's pish.

Tony If you feel the need tay say something tay the girl, you say it.

Stevie I will.

Tony But remember, it's all about perception.

Stevie Is it?

Tony I went out with this girl once – well, she wasnay really my bird, more ay a . . .

Stevie Hing?

Tony Aye. More ay a hing, ken.

Stevie Aye.

Tony But this girl she thought she looked a bit like Princess Diana. Well, she used tay tell me all the time that people told her she looked like Princess Diana. And tay be fair they did.

Beat.

Me, I thought she was more verging on the Myra Hindley than the Lady Di.

Beat.

It's perception.

Beat.

There's a fine line between the Queen of Hearts and Saddleworth Moor.

Pause.

Stevie I better go and see how she is.

Tony Aye, you better.

Stevie exits. Tony smiles to himself. He takes a drink. Wanders around the living room until he comes to the coffin. He stares at it. He turns away. Walks a few paces. Stops. Turns around. Looks at the coffin. Goes back to it and opens it a touch. Nikki enters. Tony reaches into the coffin to touch Andy. He suddenly becomes aware of Nikki. Startled, he jumps back from the coffin but the lid slams on his fingers.

Tony (*in pain*) Fuck.

Nikki Shit.

Tony (*hopping around holding his fingers*) Fucking hell.

Nikki Shit.

Tony Fucking bastard.

Nikki Was it sore?

Tony My fucking nail.

Nikki Press it.

    Nikki grabs Tony's hand and presses the nail.

Tony (*in pain*) Fuck.

Nikki keeps hold of his hand and presses again. Tony screams.

Nikki It's the only way.

Tony Fucking hell.

Nikki (*presses even harder*) You'll lose it otherwise.

Tony Ooowww . . . you fucking bitch.

Nikki (*presses*) Excuse me?

Tony Aaaahhhh.

    Beat.

Have you no' got any ice?

Nikki You don't need ice.

Tony No?

Nikki (*she squeezes again*) Not if you're a man about it.

Tony squeals.

This is much better.

Beat.

My dad taught me this.

Tony CIA was he?

Nikki Joiner.

Tony (*in pain*) Jesus!

Nikki Nothing like Jesus.

Beat.

Doesn't have a beard for one. But he was always hitting his nails and stuff. And this it's what's best, he says.

Tony goes down on his knees.

Nikki I know it's sore. And I know men aren't good with pain. But it's like any pain, it's worth it in the long run.

Nikki lets go of his hand.

Tony Thank you.

Nikki (*indicates the coffin*) Were you saying goodbye?

Tony Ay?

Nikki To . . . (*Indicates the coffin.*)

Tony Oh . . . eh . . . yeah.

Beat.

Absolutely.

Beat.

I just wanted to, you know . . .

Nikki Touch him?

Tony No.

Pause.

So what's it like to be back?

Nikki It's nice.

Tony Yeah.

Beat.

Nothing's changed.

Nikki It's reassuring.

Tony Aye.

Beat.

Because the last time I was home the place seemed really well off. It's shit coming back to somewhere that everybody seems to have done well for themselves. That's not the proper homecoming scenario.

Nikki You should be returning as a hero.

Tony Everyone should be doing shite.

Nikki Spreading largesse among the downtrodden of the parish.

Tony It was disturbing.

Nikki Well, don't worry, according to my sister it was all just jiggery-pokery with numbers.

Tony Good.

Nikki But then the whole world's just jiggery-pokery with numbers.

Tony I prefer it when Scotland's poor.

Pause.

So what do you do, to stop yourself being poor?

Nikki Marvellous, isn't it?

Tony What?

Nikki After all these years . . . it still comes round to what do you do for a living?

Tony Well, a man's got to ponce off someone?

Nikki Suppose.

    Pause.

I work for the Scottish Executive. Or Government, as it now is.

Tony Really?

Nikki Yeah.

Tony See, I had you down as a pole-dancer.

Nikki I am.

Tony For the Scottish Executive?

Nikki Government.

Tony Government.

Nikki It's new. Part of 'Creative Scotland'.

Tony Fantastic. I fucking love the arts.

Nikki You can't beat a bit of culture.

Tony Soon as I walked in the door. Saw your frame.

    Touches her upper arm.

That muscle tone.

    Moves his hand towards her leg.

Those legs.

Nikki pulls away from him.

Tony I said, wow, she's definitely a civil servant.

Pause.

So what are you wearing to the funeral?

Nikki I don't know.

Beat.

Something inappropriate?

Tony What the fuck's inappropriate these days?

Nikki (*indicates coffin*) It's what he would have wanted.

Pause.

I'm not really a lap-dancer.

Tony No?

Nikki It's aerospace I'm in.

Tony Aerospace?

Nikki Yeah.

Tony Planes and shit.

Nikki Missiles and shit.

Beat.

R and D.

Beat.

Research and development.

Tony Really?

Nikki Yeah.

Pause.

Tony I couldn't do that.

Nikki No Highers?

Tony No, I mean how do you feel when you watch the news and see them being fired?

Nikki It's like watching your kids going off to school.

Beat.

Which is ironic, because a lot of them do actually veer off course and hit schools. Orphanages usually. But then again it's more work for R and D to try and stop them homing in on the blind orphans.

Beat.

I reconcile myself morally to it by telling myself that because most of what we fire is at the Third World, they're all probably unhappy anyway.

Tony Nobody misses them.

Nikki I'm sending them to a happier place.

Beat.

What about yourself?

Tony I build car parks.

Nikki Another builder?

Tony I have a company that does it.

Nikki A building company?

Tony We build them at airports usually.

Nikki Is there a future in that? Cars and airports?

Tony It doesn't matter whether there's a future in it, all that matters is if there's a now in it.

Nikki You're not one for the long game?

Tony Is there a future in anything?

Nikki Boats.

Tony Aye. Yeah. Big future in boats I suppose.

Nikki And weapons. Huge future for weapons.

Tony Suppose.

Nikki And my big idea.

Tony You have a big idea?

Nikki Turning humans into oil.

Tony Wow.

Nikki Too many humans, not enough oil. Turn the humans into oil.

Tony When you say it, it seems really obvious.

Nikki Some sort of big compress ought to do the trick.

SCENE FOUR

Vicky and Stevie are in the bedroom.

Stevie Did you manage to sleep?

Vicky A little bit.

Stevie Good.

Beat.

Good.

Beat.

Sleep is good.

Pause.

You should try and rest.

Vicky I can't.

Stevie Rest is good.

Vicky I'm not tired.

Stevie No?

Vicky No.

Stevie Yeah, big day tomorrow, though.

Beat.

You'll need to be rested.

Pause.

Vicky How was it?

Stevie How was what?

Vicky Seeing your pal.

Stevie Tony?

Vicky Yes. Tony. The guy downstairs. The one you picked up from the airport. Your pal.

Pause.

Stevie It was a'right.

Vicky Alright?

Stevie Aye.

Vicky You haven't seen the guy for years and it was alright?

Stevie Yeah . . .

Vicky One of your best pals?

Pause.

Stevie It was good.

Vicky Good.

Stevie He's fine.

Vicky Good.

Pause.

Stevie Good.

Beat.

Aye.

Beat.

Fine.

Pause.

Vicky Did you catch up?

Stevie Aye.

Vicky What did you catch up about?

Stevie Loads ay things ay.

Vicky Like what?

Stevie Oh . . . just the usual ay . . .

Beat.

Pish.

Vicky Pish?

Stevie Aye. Same old Tony ay. Blethering pish.

Vicky So your pal that you haven't seen for years comes halfway round the world to the funeral of one of your best pals and you blether pish to each other.

Stevie Well it's expected ay.

Pause.

66

Vicky He's hasn't aged very well, has he?

Stevie Who?

Vicky Tony.

Stevie Hasn't he?

Vicky He looks terrible. Well, not terrible. I mean, compared to before.

Stevie Well, you know, he is older.

  Beat.

We all are.

  Pause.

I thought you didn't know him before?

Vicky I didn't.

  Beat.

I just . . . eh . . . I saw a photo . . . once.

Stevie Just the once?

Vicky Yeah.

  Nods.

He was gorgeous.

  Beat.

I mean, I'm all for wooing a girl and that, but fuck me, when you look like that, then you get to . . .

  Beat.

Fuck me.

  Pause.

Stevie?

Stevie Yeah?

Vicky I have to confess something to you.

Stevie No, you don't.

Vicky I do.

Stevie You don't.

Vicky I'm really sorry.

Stevie It's okay.

Vicky No. I'm really sorry.

Stevie It's fine.

Vicky I do kind of know him.

Stevie Oh!

Vicky I'm sorry.

Stevie No. I mean . . . it's okay.

Vicky No, it's not.

Stevie It is.

Vicky It's not.

Stevie You don't need to worry about . . . that . . . now.

Vicky What has he said?

Stevie Nothing.

Vicky Really?

Stevie Yeah.

Vicky It was a long time ago.

Stevie That's fine then.

Vicky It was stupid. And I really wish I hadn't.

Stevie It's fine.

Vicky I didn't have like a relationship with him or anything.

Stevie It's fine.

Vicky Really?

Stevie Of course.

Vicky Thanks.

    Pause.

He was really nice.

Stevie (*smiles*) Was he?

Vicky Gorgeous.

Stevie Okay.

Vicky Sorry.

Stevie What?

Vicky I shouldn't have said that?

Stevie No.

Vicky I shouldn't have.

Stevie It's fine.

Vicky It's not fine.

Stevie Well, I feel fine.

    Pause.

Vicky He was nice, too. You wouldn't have believed how nice he was. A bit too nice maybe for how he looked.

    Beat.

Oh shit, I shouldn't be saying this. Should I?

Stevie It's okay.

Vicky No. These are terrible things to say. I'll be saying you would have really liked him next.

Pause.

But you do really like him.

Beat.

He's your mate.

Stevie No. (*Indicates coffin.*) Andy was my mate.

Pause.

Vicky Please don't worry.

Beat.

I would never let people who know you know something you don't.

Beat.

I know you would hate that.

(*Picks up the bottle from the table.*) Do you want a tranquilliser?

Stevie No.

Vicky And don't worry, it wasn't the sex either.

Stevie What wasn't?

Vicky He wasn't all kind and gentle. Not like you.

Stevie Shoosh.

Vicky He was all . . . chunky.

Stevie Save your strength . . .

Vicky A chunky man.

Stevie For tomorrow.

Vicky I shouldn't be telling you this, should I?

Stevie No.

Vicky I'm sorry.

Stevie I'm okay.

Vicky I'm stressed. My husband . . . my fiancé . . . my boyfriend . . . my . . .

Whatever you are.

Stevie I know.

Pause.

Vicky Don't worry. It's nothing to do with you and me. I love you Stevie. I don't even know Tony. Not really. Nothing's going to happen.

Beat.

And even if it did, he would just be . . . a hate-fuck.

Beat.

And I'm not into hate-fucks.

Stevie Not unless they're part of a long-term, loving relationship.

Vicky (*pats his arm*) You need to be secure about that.

Stevie I am secure.

Beat.

Now.

Beat.

Definitely.

Vicky You should be, though. Because even if I did . . . It would just be . . .

Mimes a violent thrust.

like . . .

Groans ecstatically.

It wouldn't be . . .

Whimpers pathetically.

like you . . .

Beat.

your . . .

Beat.

. . . love.

Stevie Good.

Beat.

I'm glad.

Vicky We need to be honest with each other.

Stevie I know.

Vicky With everybody around us.

Stevie Aye.

Vicky That's how we got in this mess in the first place.

Stevie Aye.

Vicky Are you going to agree with everything I say?

Stevie Yes.

Vicky Why?

Stevie I'm very agree . . . mentative.

Vicky Is that a word?

Stevie It is now.

Vicky Honesty.

Stevie All the way.

Vicky No lies.

Stevie Absolutely.

Vicky I hate lies.

Stevie Me too.

SCENE FIVE

Tony and Nikki are in the living room.

Nikki Do you want a drink?

Tony I'm off the drink at the moment.

Nikki You were drinking earlier?

Tony I was being polite.

Nikki I know people say you shouldn't seek refuge in the booze at a time like this. But I like the booze.

Beat.

You don't like the booze?

Tony I do like the booze, yes. Just not at the moment.

Nikki Why?

Tony It's just, it's . . . it's so fucking popular, you know? It was one thing when it was just the interesting, talented people who were alkies. But now it's everybody.

Nikki I fucking love the booze.

Takes a long drink.

Oh yes. A very big fan of the booze, me.

Tony It's expected now. The female of the species is much drunker than the male.

Nikki Don't you approve? Of the booze for girls?

Tony God, no.

Beat.

I'm all for it. I think it's heroic.

Nikki Thank you.

Tony My only worry is that you need to give some thought to leaving us an activity where we still think we can outdo you. You've robbed us of our dominance in every other sphere and now you're even outdoing us in the drink.

Nikki spots the cocaine on the table, sits down and picks up the twenty and takes a line.

Tony I mean you don't want to back us into a corner, do you?

Nikki Are you feeling backed into a corner?

Tony No.

Nikki You sure?

Nikki offers the note to Tony. He shakes his head.

You're not partial?

Tony I don't mind it.

Nikki You don't approve.

Tony No, don't get me wrong. I'm all for it. It just doesn't seem to agree with me. I snort it, or even dab it, and I just get all like mucusy, you know.

Nikki Nice.

Tony The next couple of days it's like I've got the flu.

Nikki I find it really agrees with me. The yayo.

Tony Well, you are a young 'un.

Nikki So you don't drink, you don't take drugs . . .

Tony Not after what happened to Andy.

Nikki I wouldn't be too upset about that.

Tony No?

Nikki No.

Tony It's a shame for your sister?

Nikki Do you think?

Tony Yeah.

Pause.

Nikki Fuck Vicky.

Tony You're bad.

Nikki I didn't say that.

Tony I heard you not saying it.

Nikki No, I mean, I didn't mean it.

Tony I hope not.

Nikki What I mean is. You know. It doesn't have to be the sole topic of conversation, does it?

Tony No.

Nikki Shit happens.

Tony It definitely does.

Pause.

Nikki I wouldn't worry about her. She'll be fine.

Tony I tell you, when it's me, they better be pulling my body through the streets behind a thousand oiled poledancers.

Nikki You subscribe to the pharaonic school of burial?

Tony I do, aye.

Nikki Wailing and gnashing of teeth?

Tony Fucking right. You pop your clogs, then so does the missus, the family, friends, acquaintances – all get put in there with you. The pyramid gets bricked up and that's your lot.

Nikki Solves the left-behind problem.

Tony No moping, no misery, no nothing.

Nikki But unfortunately, due to the authorities deeming it economically wasteful, everybody has to go through the motions.

Tony You've got to go through the motions.

Nikki Then no one gets suspicious.

Tony Should we be suspicious?

Nikki Well, it's a funny thing.

   Beat.

Can I let you into a little bit of a secret?

Tony Of course you can.

Nikki This goes no further.

Tony Absolutely.

Nikki I really mean it.

Tony Discretion is my middle name.

Nikki That's an unusual middle name.

Tony Unusual but apt.

Nikki She's not really that bothered. Vicky.

Tony Not really that bothered?

Nikki I mean she's sad.

Tony Of course.

Nikki But I think she was beginning to dread the thought of spending the rest of her life with him.

Tony She was gonna spend the rest of her life with him?

Beat.

But they were only getting married?

Pause.

Sorry. I couldn't resist it.

Nikki The old ones are the best.

Pause.

Tony Do you think I look old?

Nikki Yeah.

Tony (*laughs*) No. Seriously?

Nikki Yeah.

Beat.

Seriously.

Pause.

Tony Too old for you?

Nikki Too . . . many different . . . things for me.

Pause.

But it's nice that Vicky and Stevie are going to get together. There's not such a gap there.

Tony So they are, are they?

Nikki I think so.

Tony He did say something, yeah, about the correct passage of time to keep things respectable.

Nikki Fuck it, I say. Bash on.

Tony Aye, I'm in the same dinghy with you on that, like.

Nikki Who cares about other people?

Tony The one person that would've cared's gone.

Nikki Exactly.

Tony If it makes her happy?

Nikki (*indicates coffin*) It's what he would've wanted.

SCENE SIX

Vicky and Stevie are in the bedroom.

Vicky So did you mention it to him?

Stevie What?

Vicky About us?

Stevie Us.

Vicky Us.

   Beat.

To Tony?

Stevie I kinday mentioned it to him.

Vicky Kinday?

Stevie Aye.

   Beat.

Kinday.

Vicky How can you kinday mention something?

Stevie I didn't go into details.

Vicky I didn't want you to go into details.

Stevie I didn't go into details.

Vicky Good.

Stevie At all.

Vicky I'm glad you didn't.

Stevie I'm glad you're glad I didn't.

Vicky I wanted you to test the water.

Stevie That's what I did.

Vicky Good.

Stevie I tested the water.

> *Beat.*

Without going into details.

> *Pause.*

Vicky And what did he say?

Stevie He didn't really say anything.

Vicky No?

Stevie No.

> *Pause.*

Vicky Oh.

Stevie It was more his . . . demeanour.

Vicky His demeanour?

Stevie Aye.

Vicky And how was his demeanour?

Stevie I wouldn't say he approved.

Vicky No?

Stevie He didnay really disapprove either.

Vicky He didn't?

Stevie I dinnay really ken, though. It was confusing.

Vicky How?

Stevie He was talking about perspective.

Vicky Perspective?

Stevie Perception.

  Beat.

The way I could be perceived.

Vicky The way you're perceived?

Stevie The way we would be perceived by other people.

Vicky I thought you didn't care about other people.

Stevie Princess Di.

Vicky Princess Diana?

Stevie And Myra Hindley.

Vicky Myra Hindley?

Stevie People think they're Princess Di but they look like Myra Hindley.

Vicky What?

Stevie Or something.

Vicky He thinks I look like Myra Hindley?

Stevie No . . .

Vicky Cheeky bastard.

Stevie No.

Vicky (*looking in mirror*) I look nothing like Myra Hindley.

Stevie Or Princess Diana.

Pause.

Look, I'm not really sure what his point was . . . he just said I should be careful. We should be careful. At the moment.

Pause.

Vicky Maybe I should talk to him?

Stevie I think you should maybe wait a wee bit.

Vicky Why?

Stevie Well, he's down there with your sister.

Vicky Is he?

Beat.

Doing what?

Stevie Talking, I think?

Vicky Talking? With my sister?

Beat.

That'll be right.

Stevie Yeah. He did say . . . you know?

Vicky What?

Stevie She's a very good-looking girl.

Vicky What about me?

Stevie So are you.

Pause.

She is really fucking lovely though.

Beat.

I mean it has to be said ay?

Pause.

Vicky No.

Pause.

Stevie I've never been good at this.

Beat.

Never been good at it. Even when I was younger I couldn't do girls. Women. I was rubbish at it. I wasn't funny. I wasn't charming. I wasn't . . . anything.

Beat.

But at least I was . . .

Vicky Young?

Stevie Then you get older. And you dinnay ken what folk like any more. What they want from you. You get confused.

Beat.

I'm confused.

Vicky Confusion isn't attractive.

Stevie It's no'.

Pause.

Vicky I'm going to go and speak to Tony.

Stevie I'll come with you?

Vicky No. I want to talk to him alone.

Stevie It's nothing to do with him.

Pause.

Listen, I like the guy. Dinnay get me wrong. He's one of my pals. My very best pals . . .

Vicky I know that.

Stevie He was.

Vicky Is?

Stevie Was.

Beat.

He's an arse. He's a bawbag. But I mean, you ken what he's like. You don't mind. He's still your friend. We all kent what he was like ay. You ken what folk like him are like. He's going to have a go at your woman at some point.

Beat.

And lassies . . . he's a legend. He gets everyone. He's magic with the girls.

Pause.

There's things that happen in the world because they do ay. There's no point in getting your knickers in a twist about them. Some things just are what they are. And one of those things is . . . is that you cannay compete with some folk. There's a hierarchy. I ken there's a fucking hierarchy like. I ken that. In fact, I like the fact there's a fucking hierarchy. I like it. I'm all in favour ay a pecking order. And I was always quite happy with my place in the pecking order. I didn't mind. But not now.

Beat.

I love you.

Vicky I know.

Pause.

And don't worry.

Beat.

You had me a bawbag.

SCENE SEVEN

Tony and Nikki are in the living room.

Tony So what about you?

Nikki What about me?

Tony What's your story?

Nikki Nothing much.

Tony Got a bloke?

Nikki I've got several, thank you.

Tony That's a shame.

Nikki It's a bugger, innit.

Tony I was getting ready to throw it all away for you there if you hadn't.

Nikki Were you?

Tony Oh aye. I was that far away.

(*Shrugs.*) Might as well have a drink now.

Nikki I'll get us another.

Nikki exits to get the drinks. Tony starts to chop out some lines. He takes a line. Nikki re-enters. She gives Tony his drink.

Tony I chopped you out another cheeky wee line there.

Nikki goes to take the line. As she leans forward her hair gets in her way. Tony holds it back for her with both hands.

Nikki Thanks.

Nikki takes the line.

Tony I like your hair.

Nikki Thanks.

She sits back up, handing the note to Tony.

It grows out of my head.

Tony Excellent.

Pause.

Nikki You can let go now.

Tony (*he lets her hair go*) Sorry.

Nikki 'S alright.

Tony And is that your natural colour?

Nikki That's very . . . bold.

Tony Bold's my middle name.

Nikki I thought it was 'Discretion'?

Pause.

Tony So is it? Your natural colour?

Nikki And why would you need to know that?

Tony It's my job.

Nikki I thought you parked cars?

Tony My other job.

Nikki Oh.

Tony It's only part time but it's quite specialised. It's very specialised, well, under-cover really, for the Government.

Nikki Like James Bond?

Tony It's not really spying, I mean I was recruited when I was at Cambridge obviously, but it's more, well . . . I assess and, eh . . . verify, the natural hair colour of the female population.

Nikki I've never heard of that job before.

Tony It's very important.

Nikki It must be.

Tony The census figures for one thing. You know, you can't have a country claiming a certain percentage of brunettes when all the time they're quite obviously not.

Nikki And do you enjoy your work?

Tony Well, it's no picnic. The whole assessment process can, well, it can take hours sometimes.

Nikki Are you very thorough?

Tony I am.

Beat.

That's what I'm known for, at the agency, my thorough-ness. I'm there and I don't budge till I know, one way or the other.

Pause.

Nikki You couldn't tell with me.

Beat.

Too well-groomed.

Tony That's something that's slipped past me here. This grooming thing.

Nikki It's what men want nowadays.

Tony I dinnay get it. I think it's to do with having kids ay. You get confronted by a bald fanny your first instinct is to put a nappy on it.

Nikki Generation gap.

Tony You're the only thing I miss about back here.

Nikki Me?

Tony The girls.

Beat.

There's very few things I'd go to war for. But I'd fucking fight anyone who tried to deny women round here the right to wear hardly anything, get pissed and sleep with everybody.

Nikki That's so sweet.

Tony I'm practically chivalrous.

Nikki You could be a crusader.

Tony That's not a good idea where I live.

Nikki They can keep their fucking oil.

Tony Just don't fucking interfere with our lassies' clothes.

Nikki Touch my Laura Mercier and you're a fucking goner.

Pause.

Tony I think most chaps who get near you are a goner.

Nikki Is that right?

Tony I reckon.

Nikki And are you most chaps?

He moves towards her to kiss her. She slips away.

Tony We have a lot in common, you and me.

Nikki We really do, don't we?

Beat.

But there's no future in long-distance relationships.

Tony No?

Nikki The carbon footprint for one thing.

Pause.

Tony I thought we were getting on?

Nikki Look. I'm home on holiday. You know what it's like when you're on holiday? You do things you wouldn't usually.

Beat.

Don't feel bad. I'm sure you were a thoroughly attractive chap in the past. In fact, I know you were.

Tony Have I still got it?

Nikki My sister told me.

Tony Oh.

Nikki I think it's admirable when somebody lets themself go as much as you have.

Points at his top.

That's a smashing jumper, though.

Tony It's Marc Jacobs.

Nikki I love Marc Jacobs.

Vicky enters.

Vicky (*to Tony*) Can I have a word?

Stevie and Nikki are in the bedroom.

Nikki No taste in men. That's always been her problem.

Pause.

Sorry.

Beat.

I feel like I need a shower.

Stevie That's T for you.

Nikki He's just a fucking . . .

Stevie Sleaze?

Nikki There's a point where it all gets a bit . . .

Stevie Threatening?

Beat.

He's got a bit of form for that.

Nikki Really?

Stevie Well, I mean, you know, when he was younger, you know, like years ago and that ay, there might have been the odd, tearful, fourteen-year-old in his flat of a Sunday morning.

Beat.

Never came to court or anything like that . . .

Shrugs.

Once the genie's out the bottle, the genie's out the bottle.

Nikki He's an arsehole.

Stevie It's no' going back in till it's had its three wishes.

Nikki You'd think he'd know better at his age.

Stevie It's worse at his age.

Beat.

At our age.

Nikki Is it?

Stevie When their powers fade, people get desperate. Then he's in a room with a girl like you . . .

Beat.

Me. I don't even speak to any girl under the age of twenty-five.

Nikki No?

Beat.

What if she speaks to you first?

Stevie I just ignore her.

Nikki What if you know them?

Stevie If I dinnay speak to them, then I cannay know them, so it works out fine.

Nikki What if she worked in a shop and you were trying to buy something?

Stevie I try not to go into shops.

Nikki What about at the checkout at a supermarket?

Stevie I always go to older women's checkouts, or boys'.

Nikki What if it was really quiet, like in the morning, and there was only one checkout and it was a really beautiful young girl and she said good morning?

Stevie I pretend I cannay get the plastic bag open. Head down, card, pin number and out the door.

Nikki That's quite ignorant.

Stevie I just dinnay want people getting the wrong end of the stick ay.

Nikki You can at least be polite.

Stevie You go in somewhere, into a shop somewhere, and there's some young lassie, then the next time you're in there, you say hello, then you know, maybe like a couple of hundred hellos later you're talking to them about other things, weather or feelings or something. Then you start going in there all the time, just to talk to them, nothing else. And then eventually they start getting worried about how you're always coming in there and staying too long, talking too much about the weather and your feelings. Then you go there one day and they won't let you in, the security guards won't let you in. Even though you just want a paper, they won't let you in. You're barred from the shop. For harassing staff. You were just being polite. They were talking to you too. They were the one that started the talking. Why would they start talking to you if they weren't interested in you? Why would they suddenly decide you were a nuisance?

Beat.

And you have to ask them these questions. You have to talk to them about it. You just want to discuss it. Reasonably. With them. But they won't let you into the shop. So you have to wait for them on their way home.

Beat.

And it's worse when it's dark because when you jump out and say, 'Don't be nervous, I just want to talk to you,' they get a fright. People don't listen when they're frightened ay, they don't listen about the weather and your feelings, they just say, 'How do you know which way I walk home?' and 'How do you know where I live?'

Then it's 'Stop crying, don't scream. I'm not going to hurt you.'

Beat.

Then you're going in the back of the van with the blanket over your head and the crowd are all chanting . . .

Impersonates an angry crowd.

Beast! Beast! Beast!

Beat.

So . . . what's it like being back in the town?

Pause.

Nikki I can't wait to get away again.

SCENE NINE

Vicky and Tony are in the living room.

Vicky How does it feel to be back?

Pause.

Tony I can't imagine how you must be feeling.

Vicky No one ever died on you?

Tony Not so far. Everybody in my family seems to enjoy rude health and prosperity *ad infinitum.*

Beat.

Sorry.

Vicky That's alright.

Pause.

Tony I suppose it makes you think about things, though.

Vicky Does it?

Tony Yeah.

Vicky I'll take your word for it.

Tony What? No thoughts about the big questions in life? No contemplation of your own mortality?

Vicky I dinnay think so.

Tony Nothing about the world you live in? About metaphysics? About what really exists? Is the world a mechanical or deterministic system or does it contain chance events or the causally inexplicable emergence of novelty?

Vicky Nut.

Beat.

But then I was off school the day we did that. I remember, I had a cold.

Pause.

So, how does it feel?

Tony (*looks at his watch*) So far?

Vicky So far?

Tony Everything's just the same.

Vicky Apart from the things that aren't.

SCENE TEN

Nikki and Stevie are in the bedroom.

Nikki D'you never just fancy getting the fuck out of Dodge?

Stevie Not really, no.

Nikki Just disappearing into the wide blue yonder?

Stevie It doesn't work like that, does it?

Nikki Doesn't it?

Stevie You can't just run away.

Nikki You can.

Stevie You can't.

Nikki It's tempting, though?

Stevie No' really.

Nikki Not even a little bit?

Stevie I've got responsibilities.

Nikki To?

Stevie My boy.

Nikki Right.

Pause.

I thought you didn't get to see him?

Stevie Aye. But . . . that's . . . that's a temporary thing.

Nikki It would be an opportunity for him as well, though?

Stevie You think?

Nikki It's good to do different things.

Stevie (*shrugs*) I've always been just the same.

Nikki I can imagine that.

Stevie Apart from when I went mental for a bit.

Nikki And how was that for you?

Stevie It was mental.

Nikki You didn't enjoy it?

Stevie No' really.

Nikki But it was a change at least?

Pause.

Stevie What about his schooling? My boy?

Nikki They've got schools in other places. I've seen them.

Beat.

Seriously though, broaden his horizons living somewhere nice.

Stevie It's good to live somewhere crap too, though.

Nikki It is?

Stevie It's character-forming.

Nikki Right.

Stevie You live somewhere shit, like here, then any bairn's gonnay rebel against it. They're going to want to get out, want to be a success. They'll jump on the first milk float out at fifteen, and by the time they're thirty they'll be Bill Gates.

Nikki I never thought of that.

Stevie There's a lot to be said for staying in the one place.

SCENE ELEVEN

Tony and Vicky are in the living room.

Tony Everybody's just the same.

Vicky I suppose if they weren't, they wouldn't tell you.

Tony Probably not.

(*Indicates coffin.*) He's getting cremated?

Vicky Yes.

Tony Was that what he wanted?

Vicky (*shrugs*) We never really discussed it.

Tony Right.

Pause.

Doing anything special . . . with the ashes?

Vicky I'm not really sure. He never really had anywhere special he liked to go or anything. He only really had his job.

Beat.

And me.

Tony What more does a man need?

Vicky I was thinking, well, he was a builder . . . and he did want to get into property development. So I was thinking of scattering them in that new housing development he was working on.

Tony laughs.

Vicky I'm serious.

Tony Oh.

Pause.

Where's that?

Vicky Bytescostan.

Tony Where's that?

Vicky By the new Tesco.

Pause.

Tony You know I'm no' being funny or anything but . . . I mean he was a great bloke and that . . .

Vicky Your best friend.

Tony But he wasn't the brightest ay.

Vicky Well, I wouldn't have wanted him on my team in *University Challenge*.

Beat.

But I mean, what d'you want? You can't have everything.

Pause.

Tony Course, you'll have to watch yourself.

Vicky Why?

Tony (*indicates the room*) All this.

Beat.

There's some blokes who'll be thinking they could be quids in.

Beat.

Some might even see you as a bit of a challenge at the moment.

Vicky Don't worry. I know.

Beat.

If I had a pound for every time someone's said, 'Anything I can do? And . . . I mean . . . anything . . . no matter what. You only have to pick up that phone.'

Pause.

They wouldn't get much out of me anyway.

Tony Good for you.

Vicky No, I mean, this isn't real. None of this belongs to us. Me. It's all on the company. And that's fucked.

Pause.

It's funny. I know it's everybody's dream. Be their own boss. Entrepeneur, all that. But it doesn't suit some people.

(*Indicates the coffin.*) He was a worker alright. But he wasn't a boss. He could work any hours, do anything. Never off a day, or let anyone down. He was a machine. But once he was in charge, once it was up to him, he couldn't do it.

Pause.

D'you ever think about how you'd like to be someone else?

Tony Eighteenth-century French aristocrat. Idle, debauched, bit of a dashing cunt. Ravish everything that moves. Posh, servants, slaves. Animal, vegetable, mineral. Drink. Drugs. Duels. Drop dead of gout and syphilis a fortnight before the revolution kicked off.

Vicky You've really thought that through.

Tony Not enough people do. That's the problem. My attitude is, you never know ay. You find a bottle on a beach, what if you give it a wipe, get your three wishes and have an attack of stage fright?

Vicky You'd never live it down.

SCENE TWELVE

Stevie and Nikki are in the bedroom.

Nikki You were with Andy . . . when he . . .

Pause.

Stevie When he died?

Nikki Yeah. When he died.

Stevie Aye. Yeah. I was. Yeah. Aye.

Pause.

Nikki And how was that?

Stevie Aye. Yeah.

Beat.

It was fine.

Beat.

Yeah. Aye.

Beat.

Fine.

Pause.

Nikki Did he say anything?

Pause.

Stevie When?

Nikki When he died?

Stevie Right. Aye. When he died. Aye. Right.

Pause.

Nikki So did he?

Stevie Say anything?

Nikki Yes!

Pause.

Stevie No.

Pause.

Not a word.

Nikki Nothing?

Stevie (*shakes his head*) Nothing.

Nikki No last words, or . . .

Stevie Like what?

Nikki I dunno. You were the one that was with him?

Stevie Aye.

  Beat.

I was. With him.

  Pause.

I was with him when he died.

  Pause.

Nikki But nothing?

Stevie No.

  Pause.

Did he say anything about you, you mean?

Nikki No.

Stevie No.

  Beat.

I mean why would he, ay.

Nikki Why would he.

Stevie There'd be no reason for him to say anything about you.

Nikki Exactly.

  Pause.

Stevie He wasnay really much of a talker, though, was he?

Nikki That's true.

Stevie Never really one for . . . chatting. Or . . .

Nikki Saying things.

Stevie He would say things. He would say things about things. Just, he wasn't really a big one for . . .

Nikki Conversation.

Stevie That wasn't really his role in the group.

Nikki People have different roles. In groups.

Stevie (*nods*) They do.

 Pause.

Nikki I don't think I ever had a conversation with him.

Stevie No?

Nikki No.

Stevie Well, dinnay worry, everybody knew what he thought of you.

Nikki What?

Stevie I mean, not what he thought of you, just, ken, what he thought of you, you know, he thought you were a ride. Obviously. I mean you are ay. You are a ride. It's a fact. And he'd known you since you were a young girl and that. And he'd obviously seen you kind ay, ken, blossoming and that ay. And he would say tay folk, ken, what a fucking ride that Vicky's wee sister hing is going to be. Not like all the time or that, not like he was a drooling, fucking, mental, sex case or anything, he would just, ken, say, if he'd been tay pick up Vicky from your house or that and he'd seen you traipsing about in your pants or whatever, he'd say tay us all, what a fucking pelt that wee hing is ay. I seen her in her pants.

101

Beat.

And dinnay worry, I dinnay think he was ever one ay they boys that was like, ken, raking through your underwear or that, ken, helping himself tay a pair ay your tiny pairs ay pants for using as a wank rag or any ay that caper. No. Nothing like that. He was a normal cunt ay, and he just would say . . . I seen her in her school uniform the day . . . or in her pants . . . sooking a lollipop . . . or I dinnay ken . . . eating a banana . . . what a fucking ride she is.

Pause.

Nikki We're all going to miss him.

SCENE THIRTEEN

Tony and Vicki are in the living room.

Tony (*points at the picture on the wall*) What's your picture?

Vicky It's not my picture.

Tony No?

Vicky No.

Tony You just assume . . . when it's decor, like.

Vicky (*indicates coffin*) Him.

Tony shakes his head.

Tony It's amazing the stuff you don't know about people when you haven't seen them for a bit?

Vicky People change.

Tony Or maybe they get less bothered about what people think of them?

Vicky Maybe.

Tony (*indicates picture*) So what is it?

Vicky It's *The Three Ages of Man*.

Tony Is it?

Vicky Titian.

  Pause.

Tony It's filth is what it is.

Vicky Filth?

Tony Filth.

Vicky Do you think?

Tony Oh aye.

Vicky Know a lot about art?

Tony I know a lot about everything.

Vicky That must come in handy?

Tony Now and then.

Vicky Only now and then?

  Pause.

So what's filthy about it?

Tony What's filthy about it?

Vicky Yeah.

Tony You don't know?

Vicky I don't.

Tony Well, I mean, this lassie here, she's a nymphomaniac obviously.

Vicky Is she?

Tony In-fucking-satiable.

    Beat.

I mean she's got two . . . two, what are they, recorders?

Vicky I don't think they're recorders.

Tony They look like recorders, you know.

    Mimes playing a recorder.

Recorders.

Vicky Lutes?

Tony Flutes sideways.

    Mimes a flute.

Flutes like that.

Vicky Lutes.

Tony Lutes?

Vicky Yeah. Lutes.

Tony A lute's like a wee guitar.

Vicky Is it?

Tony I think so.

Vicky Right.

Tony They're recorders.

Vicky I don't think they had recorders then.

Tony Well, aye, yeah but it doesn't matter, does it, it's symbolic, isn't it?

Vicky Symbolic recorders?

Tony Or metaphorical.

Vicky Metaphorical recorders?

Tony Aye.

Vicky Very swanky. I don't suppose you got much swankier in the sixteenth century than a metaphorical recorder.

Tony But what matters is . . . why the two? That's my point. What's she saying with the two of them?

Beat.

It's obvious isn't it. She's saying to the boy, she's saying, cards on the table, cards on the fucking table here, mate, if you're not up to the job, if you don't manage a good enough –

Vicky Tune?

Tony – on your recorder here . . . then I'll be needing a spare.

Beat.

No excuses. Hard week at work? Stress? Medieval diet not conducive to a healthy circulation?

Beat.

Not fucking interested, pal. If you're not up to the job . . . jog on.

Vicky Quite right too.

Tony Absolutely.

Vicky Good for her.

Tony That's fine as far as it goes.

Vicky I'm all for a woman articulating the fact that's she's sexually unsatisfied.

Tony It's not gonnay do his confidence any good, is it?

Vicky She just knows what she wants from the relationship.

Tony If anything she's making things worse.

Vicky Why couldn't a woman have it all in the sixteenth century?

Tony And that boy there.

Points to the picture.

Is that her dad? No wonder he looks pissed off. That's not how you want to see your daughter behave, is it?

Vicky Not in a field, anyway.

Tony (*points to the picture*) No wonder she's got all them bairns.

Pause.

I suppose that's one advantage . . . for yourself . . . and . . . (*Indicates coffin.*) No kids.

Vicky You think?

Tony Yeah.

Pause.

Vicky Have you got children?

Tony I do, yeah.

Pause.

Two girls.

Vicky Really?

Tony (*nods*) Abril and Isabella.

Beat.

Their mum's Spanish ay.

Vicky That's nice.

Tony She is nice.

Beat.

They are nice.

Beat.

I'm nice.

Pause.

Ten years I've been with her.

Pause.

You know, when we were young . . .

Vicky Are you not still young?

Tony Your sister doesn't think so.

Vicky Aye, but she is young.

Tony She's quite . . .

Vicky Braw?

Tony Combative.

Vicky I think that's 'cause she's clever.

Tony Young and clever.

Vicky And braw.

Pause.

Tony Fucking hell.

Vicky I know.

SCENE FOURTEEN

Stevie and Nikki in the bedroom.

Nikki I think it's shocking what you're doing.

Pause.

Stevie You don't know anything about it.

Pause.

Nikki This could be a big opportunity for her, you know?

Stevie I know.

Nikki To get away from here?

Stevie I know.

Nikki For a bit at least?

Stevie I know!

  Pause.

Nikki You don't think she should?

  Pause.

Stevie It's up to her, isn't it?

Nikki It is. But, you know, she's not really in a normal frame of mind at the moment.

Stevie Who would be?

Nikki Vulnerable is what she is.

Stevie Aye.

Nikki You wouldn't want to take advantage of someone who was vulnerable, would you?

Stevie I wouldn't.

  Beat.

No.

Nikki And you don't think you are?

Stevie No.

  Pause.

Nikki You know, if you back off and give her a bit of time, she'll probably come back here and get together with you?

Stevie No, she won't.

Nikki She might.

Stevie Listen, I know this doesn't look good.

Nikki It looks awful.

Stevie I know, but you have to realise that me and your sister have always been really friendly and when all that stuff happened with my missus, all the madness, she was the one person who was always there to help. I could come and stay here, I could get away from everything. She listened to me

Nikki And Andy was here too?

Stevie Aye.

Nikki So maybe she was doing it because you were his friend?

  Pause.

Stevie No.

Nikki Why not?

Stevie 'Cause it wasn't that.

Nikki How do you know?

Stevie I know.

Nikki You don't know.

Stevie I do know.

Nikki No one knows anything about why people do things.

Stevie Aye, they do.

Nikki So why are you doing this?

Stevie Because I'm . . .

Nikki Desperate?

Stevie No. I'm . . .

Nikki A desperate, sad little man who fucks a grieving woman when she's at her lowest ebb?

Stevie You don't know anything about me. About your sister and me, the things we've said to each other, the things . . .

Beat.

You don't know anything.

Beat.

I'm one of the good guys.

Nikki You're one of the good guys?

Stevie Aye.

Nikki Nobody who says they're a good guy is ever a good guy.

Stevie I haven't done anything.

Nikki He's not even buried yet?

Stevie It was all over between them.

Nikki They were getting married tomorrow?

Stevie She wasn't . . . committed.

Nikki She –

Stevie Not a hundred per cent.

Nikki She's –

Stevie It's none of your business.

Nikki She's my sister. I love her.

Stevie So do I.

SCENE FIFTEEN

Tony and Vicky are in the living room.

Tony I always thought he was indestructible.

Pause.

I mean, we were all nutters. The things we used to do. I think back. Fucking hell. All the scrapes and nonsense.

Beat.

He was right good at fighting.

Vicky Well, that's something.

Tony Yeah. Big ay. And fucking strong tay. Way some folk ay you knew you couldnay rely on them, but no' with him. He'd always look out for you.

Shakes his head.

I don't know how we never got killed sometimes.

Pause.

Suddenly, it all seems so long ago.

Pause.

He always went out with tangy women too ay.

Vicky He did.

Tony I mean, I dinnay want tay speak out of turn or anything, but he shagged everybody.

Vicky When you're young . . .

Tony Everybody does it.

Vicky Sex and violence.

Tony You cannay beat it.

Vicky You're better at the violence and we're better at the sex.

Tony Do you think so, do you?

Vicky Definitely.

Pause.

Tony So, do you want a fight?

Vicky With you?

Tony Aye.

Vicky I haven't been in a fight in years.

Tony Who're you kidding?

Pause.

You're lucky, you know?

Vicky Lucky?

Tony Not lucky. You're . . .

Vicky Unlucky?

Tony Fortunate.

Vicky I'm glad you think so.

Tony You get another roll of the dice for free.

Vicky For free?

Tony Not for free, but, you know, don't knock it. A lot of people wouldn't mind being in your shoes.

Vicky If he was alive no one would be funny about me leaving him. I would just be moving on. So what? It happens to everybody.

Tony This is an opportunity for you. You can do whatever you want.

Beat.

And believe me there'll be no shortage of takers.

Pause.

Vicky I look awful.

Tony You do not look awful.

Vicky I do.

Tony You really don't.

He pulls her against him.

I'd say you look even better than you used to.

Vicky It must be grief.

Tony (*he runs his hand down her side*) You never felt like this –

Vicky Grief.

Tony I remember.

Vicky Or the gym.

Tony You were one of those fucks you never get out of your mind.

Vicky You've got to make the effort.

Tony I remember everything.

Vicky I did always wonder . . .

Tony (*he runs his hands over her breasts*) Your tits.

Vicky What you would look like?

Tony (*he turns her around and pulls her against him*) Your arse.

Vicky What you would be like?

Tony You were fucking amazing.

Vicky I seem to remember you being a lot taller?

Tony Ay?

Vicky I'm not mixing you up with someone else?

Beat.

You are Anthony Thomson? From the flats?

Tony Aye.

Vicky So you are the right one.

Pause.

Tony (*indicates coffin*) I sometimes wish my wife was dead.

Vicky (*pulls away from him*) You do?

Tony You know what it's like when you're married?

Vicky No. I don't.

Tony Technicalities aside. What do you think when you meet someone you want to fuck?

Vicky I don't think.

Tony You don't think?

Vicky I just fuck them.

Tony I remember.

Pause.

Well, I think. I think about my wife. I think, if you were just dead for a day, if you were just dead.

Beat.

I could do this.

Vicky It's a bit drastic.

Tony Is it?

Vicky Dead?

Tony Aye.

Vicky What about, I dunno, at work?

Tony When I look at my wife, I wish she was dead. Well, not wish she was dead . . . think . . . if only she was dead. I don't wish it, I think it.

Vicky There's a difference?

Tony Yeah.

Beat.

I think so.

Vicky And does this happen a lot?

Tony Just at that moment that some other girl gives me the come-on.

Vicky Not often, then.

Tony No.

Vicky And does she know? Your wife? About your wish?

Tony You're joking.

Beat.

She'd kill me.

Pause.

Vicky So what about . . . Immaculada and Concepcion at that moment?

Tony Who?

Vicky Your kids? I forget their names.

Pause.

Tony Kids have nothing to do with fucking.

Pause.

So how come you said you didn't know me? When I came in?

Vicky How come?

Tony Yeah.

Vicky Because . . . when you came in . . .

Tony You didn't know what to do?

Vicky You look different.

Tony We all look different.

Pause.

Vicky Maybe, I was embarrassed.

Tony Embarrassed?

Vicky I'd told my sister that you were . . .

Tony What?

Vicky Nothing.

Pause.

Tony If anybody should be embarrassed about anything it's you getting together with that fucking loser.

Vicky Stevie?

Tony Aye.

Vicky He's your friend.

Tony He's an arsehole.

Pause.

But I wish you every happiness.

SCENE SIXTEEN

Nikki and Stevie are in the bedroom.

Stevie Listen, I understand you feel like you want to protect her, I understand that, but it's up to your sister what happens now. I'm not forcing her to do anything. I'm not coercing her or taking advantage of her. I just have to do what I feel is right for me and hope that what's right for me is right for her in the end.

Beat.

This is my last chance of happiness here. I have to do everything I can to try and make her stay, because I . . .

Beat.

I just don't want to lose her.

Pause.

And there's nothing you can say to make me leave her alone.

Nikki Not even for a bit?

Stevie (*shakes his head*) I can't.

Pause.

Nikki What if I suck your cock?

Pause.

Stevie The now?

Nikki kneels in front of Stevie.

Nikki Right now.

Pause.

Stevie Okay.

Nikki (*begins to undo his belt*) And you'll leave her alone?

Stevie Can I come in your mouth?

Nikki (*she stops*) Swear you'll leave her alone.

Stevie I will.

Nikki Swear?

Stevie I swear.

Beat.

Honest.

Beat.

Fuck her.

Nikki undoes his belt and begins to undo his trousers.

Stevie (*stops her*) Actually . . .

Nikki What?

Stevie Does it have to be the now?

Nikki Yes. It has to be the now. Of course it has to be the fucking now. I don't intend on seeing you ever again, so . . .

Nikki unzips his trousers.

Stevie (*stops her*) I'll see you tomorrow?

Nikki Listen, I'm quite drunk and I've had some coke and tranquillisers.

Pulls his trousers down to his knees.

It has to be now.

Stevie But tomorrow . . .

Nikki I'll be sober tomorrow.

Stevie What if someone comes in?

Nikki Nobody's coming in.

Stevie (*pulls his trousers back up*) I think I can hear someone coming.

They both listen.

Nikki I don't hear nothing.

Nikki pulls his trousers down.

Stevie The thing is . . .

Nikki WHAT?

Pause.

Stevie I never really had time to have a shower today.

Beat.

Or yesterday.

Nikki (*sits back on her heels*) Oh.

Stevie I don't really know how clean it's going to be.

Nikki Right.

Stevie It does get a bit . . .

Nikki No.

Stevie And I wouldn't want you to have to . . .

Nikki No.

Stevie Not when it's . . .

Nikki (*stands up*) No.

Stevie If you wait till tomorrow?

Nikki Listen . . .

Stevie (*he makes a scrubbing motion*) I can give it a bit of a scrub.

Nikki No.

Stevie (*he makes a scrubbing motion*) Get myself spruced up for you?

Nikki No!

Stevie (*he does the scrubbing motion again*) You sure?

Nikki Stop doing that!

Stevie What?

Nikki (*makes a scrubbing motion*) The scrubbing . . . thing.

    Pause.

Why didn't you have a shower?

Stevie I don't know.

Nikki You were going out. Don't you wash when you're going out?

Stevie Aye.

Nikki That's what people do.

Stevie Aye.

    Beat.

I wasnay expecting this though ay. I mean, you're fucking gorgeous.

    Pause.

Nikki Listen . . .

    Pause.

You do what you want, with Vicky. Okay.

    Beat.

I'm not going to . . . let's just forget about this whole . . .

    Beat.

It didn't happen.

Stevie No?

Nikki No.

Pause.

And you have my blessing.

Nikki exits.

Stevie Yeah, but listen, tomorrow, we could . . .

Stevie exits after her.

SCENE SEVENTEEN

Tony and Vicky are in the living room.

Vicky Do you think . . .

Pause.

Tony Do I think what?

Pause.

Vicky Do you think, on the stag night . . .

Tony I didn't go on the stag night.

Vicky That's right.

Tony Don't like that sort of stuff.

Vicky No?

Tony They said they had a good time . . .

Vicky So how many prostitutes do you think he slept with?

Tony They're far too expensive to sleep with. It's fifty euros for fifteen minutes.

Beat.

You don't want to be sleeping at those prices.

Vicky I thought that's what stag nights were all about?

Tony Yeah. But, he wouldn't do that.

Pause.

And there's much more to Amsterdam than the hoors, you know?

Beat.

There's the . . . the Van Gogh Museum.

Pause.

And the . . . canals.

Beat.

Did he enjoy a canal?

Pause.

It's all for show anyway. Most lads'll say I'm off to do this and that and then they just go in and have a chat or they walk round the block and come back in and say fucking hell you want tay have seen me blah, blah, blah, blah.

Beat.

That wasn't his style.

Pause.

That's how I was so shocked when I heard about what happened on the plane.

Pause.

Vicky When he collapsed?

Tony Him being with the stewardess, I mean . . . fuck.

Long pause as Tony looks into the coffin.

You okay?

Pause.

Vicky Yeah.

Pause.

Tony Whose idea was it for him to wear this gear?

Turns to look at Vicky.

He looks fucking ridiculous.

Vicky Doesn't he?

Tony You don't like it?

Vicky I hate it.

Tony I thought you chose it?

Vicky Who told you that?

Tony Stevie.

Vicky No.

Pause.

My dress was nice.

Tony I bet it was.

Vicky It was lovely.

Beat.

Really lovely.

Nikki enters.

Vicky Do you want to see it?

Tony What?

Vicky My dress.

Stevie enters.

It's really nice.

123

Tony I'm sure it is.

Stevie Vicky?

Vicky (*to Tony*) You should really see it.

She moves to the stairs.

Come on.

Beat.

Now.

Vicky goes up the stairs. Tony hesitates, looks at Stevie.

Tony Sorry, pal.

He follows Vicky up the stairs.

SCENE EIGHTEEN

Morning. Nikki is in the living room, ready for the funeral. She is holding the bottle of tranquillisers. Vicky enters, also ready for the funeral.

Nikki You look lovely.

Vicky Thank you.

Pause.

Nikki You look like . . . you.

Vicky Well, you know . . .

Beat.

I am expected.

Vicky walks around the living room.

Vicky You could have tidied up.

Nikki It's only a couple of glasses.

Vicky Did you get rid of the . . .

Nikki Don't worry.

Sniffs.

That's all long gone.

Nikki smiles at her, looks around, finds a glass of wine and drinks from it.

Vicky Did you sleep?

Nikki Don't be daft.

Vicky At all?

Nikki I might have missed something.

Pause.

I hate missing things.

Vicky And are you feeling okay?

Nikki Great. Yeah.

Beat.

Spot on.

Shakes the bottle of tranquillisers.

You must be ready for one of these now?

Vicky I'm fine.

Nikki (*opens the bottle*) Positive?

Vicky Absolutely.

Pause.

Nikki (*takes a pill from the bottle*) I must say though, sis . . .

Gulps the pill down with a huge mouthful of wine.

I'm shocked.

Beat.

I am shocked to my core.

Beat.

And I'm pretty unshockable.

Beat.

Or at least I thought I was.

Pause.

You're some girl.

Vicky Thank you.

Nikki You are, though.

Beat.

You. Are. Some. Girl.

Beat.

That's the highest compliment I can pay you.

Vicky It's the highest compliment you can pay anyone.

Nikki I know. And you hear people say it. She's some girl. He's some boy. You hear it all the time.

Vicky Maybe too much?

Nikki It's maybe been devalued. But for you. In this instance. Right here and now. At this exact moment. Devalued or not. Nothing else fits.

Beat.

You.

Beat.

Are.

Beat.

Some.

Beat.

Girl.

Pause.

Vicky Nothing happened.

Nikki Oh, okay then.

Vicky (*walks over to the coffin*) Nothing happened.

Nikki Oh, I get it. (*Indicates coffin.*) Not in front of the corpse.

Vicky Nothing happened.

Nikki (*joins her*) He believes you.

(*Listens.*) Listen to how calm he is.

Pause.

Vicky No, it really didn't.

Nikki Excuse me, but, in my book, something happened.

Pause.

No?

Vicky He couldn't manage it.

Nikki Really?

Vicky He said he was jet-lagged.

Nikki Fuck.

Vicky If only.

Pause.

Nikki Has he not heard of Viagra?

Vicky He said it had never happened to him before.

Nikki Jet lag?

Pause.

Vicky We just talked.

Beat.

Briefly.

Nikki There's not a lot to say in that situation really.

Pause.

Were you sympathetic?

Vicky You know me, sis, I fucking hate sympathy.

Pause.

Nikki I'll give him his due. He was quite good at the talk.

Vicky He was, wasn't he?

Nikki Very good.

Vicky I was quite surprised that he failed at the action though.

Nikki That's what happens when you get good at the talk.

Pause.

Vicky People aren't good when you surprise them.

Nikki No wonder he ran off like that.

Vicky His tail . . .

Nikki Hanging . . .

Pause.

Vicky (*laughs*) Fucking hell.

Beat.

What a disaster.

Nikki It's beautiful.

Vicky What was I thinking?

Nikki I would love to know.

Vicky So would I.

Pause.

At least nobody knows.

Nikki I do.

Beat.

And you know what I'm like at keeping my mouth shut?

Vicky You better keep it shut.

Nikki It's not me you've got to worry about.

Vicky No.

Pause.

Nikki I suppose that's the end of your little understanding?

Vicky Oh, do you think so?

Pause.

Good.

Pause.

Nikki So . . . what happens now?

Pause.

Vicky We have a funeral.

Pause.

Nikki Are you not going to use your new bag?

Vicky D'you think I should?

Nikki Yeah.

Vicky It won't look like I'm celebrating?

Nikki Aren't you?

Vicky picks up her new bag and begins to fill it.

Vicky It's not a good thing, being dead.

Nikki It's not, is it?

Beat.

I'm definitely not going to do it till the end of my life.

Pause.

Vicky You know, sometimes I feel sorry for them.

Nikki Do you?

Vicky Aye.

Nikki But you hate sympathy?

Vicky Only when it's directed at me.

Pause.

I mean, what do they get?

Nikki What do they get?

Vicky Yeah.

Nikki What do we get?

Pause.

Vicky A few years of running about . . . thinking you know what you're doing. Then as soon as things change . . .

Nikki You're fucked.

Vicky walks over to the coffin and looks at it.

Vicky You only get a little bit of time.

Beat.

Then it's all over.

Pause.

It's a shame.

Pause.

Nikki Somebody should help them?

Vicky I think that's our job.

Pause.

Nikki Fuck.

Pause.

Vicky It's the only way.

The End.